From Rejection to Runway: My Immigrant Glow-Up

Verses Kindler Publication

Verses Kindler Publication.

Website: www.verseskindlerpublication.com

From Rejection to Runway: My Immigrant Glow-Up

By: Mr. Bhavik Arjun Kakkar

ISBN: 978-93-49532-33-5

1st Edition

Price: INR 249/$13

Disclaimer

From Rejection to Runway: My Immigrant Glow-Up is authored by Bhavik Arjun Kakkar. The entirety of this published work comprises the original content of the author, who has undertaken diligent efforts in its editing. The characters depicted herein may be fictitious or inspired by real events; however, they are not intended to cause offense or represent any prejudice against any caste or system. Any similarity to the names of actual individuals, locations, or institutions is purely coincidental and serves the narrative. The author bears sole responsibility for the originality of this work; the publisher assumes no liability thereof.

Index

Chapter 1: A Career Without Purpose

Growing up, I was the kind of kid who didn't have a straightforward answer to the question, "What do you want to be when you grow up? " While other children eagerly declared their ambitions to become doctors, engineers, or astronauts, I would shrug and mutter something vague about making money. My vision was financial security, the good life, and some fun along the way.

A grand career goal?
That would be a problem for the "future me" to solve. In my teenage years, such an attitude was the characteristic of my approach to life. I was not the type of student who spent hours poring through textbooks or attending extra classes with burning ambition. I had some of my best moments of living on video games.

I easily spent a whole day drowning in the glow of my computer display when I was in virtual realms to conquer challenges, which seemed to interest me more than that to be in school. A while later, I realised in truth- though I never knew it- I had two passions: games and escapism. They gave a clear sense of purpose, something real life didn't. In the virtual world, there were objectives to meet, rewards for achievement, and a sense of accomplishment in mastering a challenge. I knew what was expected and thrived on that instant gratification of success. For school, it felt endless in terms of vague expectations but with delayed rewards.

It was hard to stay motivated when the payoff seemed so far away. It wasn't that I didn't try. I'd sit at my desk, biology textbooks spread out before me and attempt to study. But my focus lasted only a short time. The diagrams of human anatomy blurred together, and the explanations felt dry and lifeless. More often than not, I'd find myself daydreaming about strategies for the next big boss fight or planning my gaming session later that night.

Biology—and, to be honest, most of my school subjects—simply couldn't compete with the thrill of gaming. My parents noticed, of course. They'd remind me of the importance of focusing on my studies, often with a mix of concern and frustration. You can't spend your life playing games," my mom would say. My dad would add, "You need to think about what you want to do, Bhavik. You can't just drift through life." I'd nod and promise to study harder, but I didn't see the urgency deep down.

I thought I had everything in the world to figure it out. Weekends were the peak of my carefree lifestyle. I would wake up late, grab breakfast, and spend the rest of the day gaming. Hours passed as I explored new levels, unlocked achievements, and connected with friends online. I loved the camaraderie of multiplayer games—how we strategised, competed, and cheered each other on.

I felt part of something meaningful in those moments, even if it was just a virtual team. School was a chore. The routines, rules, and constant pressure to perform seemed designed to stifle creativity and fun. I could have done better academically; I just didn't see the point. Without a clear career goal, studying felt like running a race without knowing where the finish line was. My teachers often told me I had potential, but I needed to learn how to use it. Potential for what?

That's a question I could never answer. My friends seemed to have the answers to everything. Some wanted to be doctors; others wanted to be engineers or software developers. They spoke as if their futures were cast in stone. I envied their certainty in their chosen vocations but could not share it in my own heart. I mumbled something vague and changed the subject whenever someone asked me what I was planning.

The reason was that I didn't have a plan, and I wasn't ready to commit. Looking back, I understand how much I clung to the simplicity of my game world. It was one place where I could feel like I was in control and where success was tangible, while failures were just opportunities to try again. In the real world, things were more complex. Expectations from my family, school demands, and uncertainty of the future weighed me down, and I wasn't prepared to bear it.

Gaming gave me a way to escape those pressures, at least for a while. Even in my free time as a teenager, there were moments when the reality of the future would creep in. I would hear my parents talk about my potential or see my friends striving for their dreams, and a pang of guilt would be there.

Subconsciously, I knew I could not sit and play video games all day. Someday, I would have to answer the question I was avoiding: What do you want to do with your life? But for now, I suppressed those thoughts. The future could wait.

I still needed to beat another level. I didn't always feel I was misbehaving. In fact, during those teenage years, I thought that's how a happy life should be: living in the moment, avoiding unnecessary stress, and doing the things you enjoy. Not that I didn't care about my studies—I just couldn't bring myself to care enough.

As far as I was concerned, life was long, and there would always be time to figure out the important stuff later. Weekdays were manageable enough. I'd go to school, sit through classes, and do the bare minimum to avoid trouble. I'd tell myself that I'd study in the evening and really focus this time, but somehow, those evenings always slipped away.

Maybe I'd open a textbook and stare at it for a while. Still, soon enough, I'd be back in my gaming chair, controller in hand, fully immersed in a world where biology diagrams didn't exist, and my biggest problem was defeating an enemy team.

As I said, on Saturday mornings, from the moment I woke up, my focused goal was set: gaming. Quickly wolfing down breakfast, I didn't say much to my parents before disappearing into my room. At lunchtime, I often looked around, remembering I hadn't moved for hours. My parents would then call me down to the table, sometimes even exasperated by my constant sitting in front of a screen.
I'd nod, promise to take a break, and then rush back to my console as soon as I finish eating.

It was not the games but the community that made me fall in love. My friends and I had created an invisible bond over our shared interest in gaming. We would spend hours strategising, arguing over tactics, and laughing at each other's mistakes. For me, those moments felt natural, more accurate than the lectures in school or the vague career advice from well-meaning relatives.

In those virtual worlds, I felt confident, capable, and, above all, free. The trouble was, though, that sense of freedom only followed me so far. It never accompanied me to the classroom or family gatherings.
I recall one evening very vividly. My dad entered my room. I was mid-game, with the headset on, fully absorbed by the screen. He waited for some time, thinking I would turn around and notice him. I finally did. He looked at me with a face I couldn't interpret. It was something between disappointment and concern.

"Bhavik," he said, "do you ever think about what you will do after school?"

I kept silent because I did not know how to speak, and I didn't want to talk about it. Eventually, I said that we would discuss this later. He sat down at the edge of my bed. "You can't keep drifting, Beta. Life is not going to wait for you to make your decision. You have to decide for your future now, not when it is already late."

I nodded, promising him I would, but we both knew it was invalid. I was not ready to start considering the future because it intimidated me. What if I wasn't able to figure it out? What if I failed? It was easy to maintain the status quo, the familiarity, the things that bring me comfort, even though I know they're not working toward anything. My mother wasn't much different. She had a more gentle approach but with the same concerns. She tried talking me through my strengths to talk me into looking into various kinds of careers. "You do well in math," she'd say. "Have you looked into engineering?" Or, "You're so creative; you might want to consider design or architecture." I appreciated the attempts on her part, but it never really made me come alive.

I did not want to find out what I was good at. I just wanted to continue doing what I liked. My friends have everything together. One friend aspired to be a doctor, and the other wanted to be a software developer. They spent their nights reading or taking extra lessons, and I looked up to their determination—even envying it—since it was alien to me.

I cringed inside when they talked of dreams and what they wanted in their futures. They were laying out the foundations of their lives, and I was confined within the present, far too frightened or obstinate to forge on. I kept my nose as close to the pavement as possible in school. I was neither a top student nor one failing miserably. Sometimes, teachers called me out for not meeting my potential, but their words became a sort of background noise to me rather than actual warnings.

I kept telling myself everything would be okay in the end and that I would figure things out when the time came.
It was a comforting lie that I clung to even as the pressure around me began to build.

Looking back, I can see how much of my teenage mindset was shaped by fear—fear of failure, fear of disappointing my parents, fear of committing to something and realising it was unsuitable for me. It was easier to avoid those fears by staying in the moment and focusing on the things that brought me immediate joy. But avoidance only works for so long. Sooner or later, life catches up.

At the time, though, I didn't know that. I thought I had all the time in the world. And so I continued playing my games, living in my bubble, believing the future could wait longer. If there's one thing I remember vividly about those years, it's how much I avoided silence. Silence meant that I had to think, and thinking meant I had to face questions I did not want answers to. Questions like my future, ambitions, or what I wanted out of this life. Instead of answers, I filled my days with noise- the sound of clicking controllers, the chatter of online friends, or just the background hum that went with a day-long gaming marathon. But the truth is, even noise can't drown out reality forever.

There were quiet, fleeting moments when the weight of everything I was avoiding would catch up to me. Sometimes, it was late at night, lying in bed after a long day of gaming, staring at the ceiling and wondering, What am I doing? Where is this going? Other times, it was when talking to my parents, and when I saw the anxiety lines etched on their faces, I couldn't help but feel guilt sneaking in as an unwelcome guest. I wasn't ignorant of their concern. My parents never lectured or scolded me, but they were disappointed in how they spoke to me—or, instead, didn't. My dad, especially, began talking less about my future and more about his past. He told me stories about his sacrifices and his risks to give our family a stable life.

He wasn't trying to guilt-trip me; I knew that.

But his words carried a weight I couldn't ignore.

It's not about being the best, Bhavik," he said one evening. "It's about knowing where you're going. You don't have to have all the answers, but you need to start asking the right questions." I didn't respond, partly because I didn't know what to say and partly because I didn't want to admit that I wasn't asking those questions—not yet. School, meanwhile, became more challenging to navigate. Not academically—I was still managing to scrape by—but socially. My friends, who shared my carefree approach to life, were starting to drift away.

They were busy with entrance exams, extra classes, and study groups.

Our conversations, once filled with jokes and gaming talk, began to shift toward plans and career goals. I felt like an outsider, stuck in a different phase of life than everyone else. I recall an especially memorable conversation that has stuck in my mind. At lunchtime, one of the friends was excitedly talking about his plans to become a mechanical engineer. He spoke with conviction, mapping out the steps he needed to take, the colleges he wanted to apply to, and the internships he hoped to land. When he turned to me and asked, "What about you, Bhavik? What's your plan?" I froze. I mumbled something about figuring it out and quickly changed the subject.

The truth was, I didn't even have a plan, and the more people asked, the more that just scared me.

As the months passed, I was further away from my peers. They were focused, driven, and purposeful while I was...floating. It wasn't that I didn't care—I did. But I felt overwhelmed every time I tried to think about the future. Where would I even start? What if I made the wrong choice? What if I failed? Those questions were paralysing, so I buried them under hours of gaming and empty distraction evening. Sitting in my room with my controller in hand, I saw myself in the mirror. I looked tired—not physically but emotionally. For the first time, I saw myself as my parents probably saw me: a teenager with potential but no direction. It was a jarring moment that forced me to confront a truth I'd been avoiding for years. I couldn't keep living like this. Something had to change.

But change was easier said than done. The idea of leaving my comfort zone and facing the unknown scared me. Gaming was safe and familiar, but the real world wasn't. Yet I knew I couldn't hide forever. I had nowhere to start, but I needed to start somewhere.

From then on, I started noticing the people around me—the people I used to call parents, teachers, and friends. I saw their hard work and their focus on their goals. It wasn't that they had everything figured out, but they were trying, which made all the difference. I realised that maybe the key wasn't having all the answers but being willing to search for them.

It wasn't like I woke up one day knowing what I wanted out of my life or where I wanted to go. But at least I began to ask myself those questions I'd been avoiding all my life. What do I want? What makes me happy? What kind of life do I want to build? They were big, scary questions, but they were a start. Those years were some of my life's most challenging and essential. They taught me it's okay to be lost if you're willing to find your way.

They taught me failure isn't the end—it's just a chance to start over. And they taught me that purpose isn't something you find overnight; it's something you build, piece by piece, one step at a time. And I sat in my room that evening, staring at a paused game on the screen, and realized my journey had barely begun. I did not know everything, but for the first time, I was prepared to start looking for them. And that, I believe, was the first step to a life of purpose.

Chapter 2: Beating Expectations

I was born into a family with the notion of measuring success based on traditional achievements. This weight of expectations became heavy for me since my grandparents had set such high standards through their long work experience as well-respected doctors. My older sister followed in their footsteps by carving out her name in the medical field. It was a legacy of discipline, perseverance, and service that my family was proud of. And, of course, they also expected me to be a part of it.

For a spectator, being part of a family like that might be inspiring. But to me, a teenager trying to find my way in life, it was choking. There was an unspoken assumption that I would take up the mantle, don a white coat, and become the next in line to carry on the tradition. It wasn't that anyone forced me outright, but the pressure was there in every conversation, every subtle glance, and every question about my future.

"Bhavik, you're good at science," my father would say, not as a suggestion but as a statement of fact. "You have it in your blood to be a doctor."

I would nod because I didn't know what to do otherwise. How could one argue against bloodline, against decades of history? How could one tell them that I'm not sure I want to be a doctor or that I need clarification about what I want?

Pressure never stopped, even when in school. Several of my classmates preferred medicine or engineering as subjects for their courses. All would attend extra coaching classes. Others read until the late hours and often discussed entrance exams and plans. They seemed so clear and focused. I envied their state of clarity but couldn't help but bring such clarity to myself.

For a long time, I tried to fit into the mould. I would tell myself that if I worked hard enough, I would feel the passion my family spoke of. I attended extra biology sessions and spent hours memorising anatomical diagrams, but the more I tried, the more I realised I was going through the motions. My heart wasn't in it.

Knowing how much my family believed in me made it more challenging. My grandparents would tell stories of their time in medical school, the struggles and triumphs, and the joy they found in helping others. My sister, already excelling in her career, would talk about her experiences with patients and how rewarding it was to make a difference in their lives. They were not trying to force me; they were trying to persuade me. But the more they said, the worse I felt.

There were instances when I wanted to succumb because it was an easier way out. My parents, relatives, and even teachers all seemed to agree on what was good for me. "Bhavik, you're smart," they would say. "You have so much potential. Don't waste it."

But deep inside of me, a small voice started saying something else. It said I didn't come to follow a specific route or find my route, even though I still needed to learn the particular way.

The first real confrontation with my family wasn't one day or night. It was over the weeks and months of frustration and unspoken tension. My parents, particularly my father, could simply not understand why I wasn't more enthusiastic about taking up medicine. To them, it was the safest, most stable career imaginable. "Why would you want to give away such a secure future?" my dad asked one evening, his voice tinged with confusion and disappointment.

I had no answer-not one they would accept anyway. How could I tell them it wasn't about security for me? Even though I loved my grandparents and sister dearly, I couldn't envision myself in their shoes. My hesitation was not due to fear or laziness. It was something far more profound, something I couldn't yet find the words for.

The discussions got more challenging with each passing day. Initially, they were peaceful discussions, my parents mildly nudging me back to the "right" track. However, with more days of indecisiveness from my side, their patience began to wear out. "Bhavik," my mom said one evening, "we are not asking you to decide today, but you must understand how important this is. Medicine is a profession that one can rely upon. It shall give you a secure life."

Her words hung in the air, heavy with expectation. I nodded, not wanting to argue, but inside, I felt suffocating. Stability. Dependability. Those words sounded like cages to me. I didn't want to live a life defined by safety and predictability—not if it meant sacrificing my aspirations.

At dinner with the family, things went from bad to worse. Dad asked me point-blank: "If not medicine, then what? What do you want to do with your life?"

I was frozen. Although I had been warned of this moment, I couldn't prepare myself for it. "I... I don't know yet," I whispered to him.

My dad shook his head, disappointment clear. "Bhavik, you can't live your life without a plan. This isn't just about you. This is about your future, about providing for yourself and your family someday. What kind of stability will you have if you don't choose a proper career?

The word stability hit me like a hammer. This was the one thing my family held dear above everything else, and this was the one thing I had no idea how to give them. But something snapped inside of me. I had been avoiding this fight for months, trying to keep everybody happy by being quiet. It was just too much anymore.

"Perhaps I don't want stability," I said, trembling with fear and rebellion. "Maybe I want to do something that makes me happy."

There was absolute silence. They just gazed at me; their faces were simply unable to read, and their eyes expressed such shock and amazement. Mom was the one who dared to talk: "Bhavik, we don't intend on stopping you from what you think or what we think for your good; that's not at all true."

I took a deep breath and tried to calm myself. "I know you do, but what's best for me might not necessarily be what you believe is best for me," I said firmly. "I need to figure this out for myself".

It was one of the most challenging conversations I had ever had. My parents weren't angry, but they were deeply hurt. I could feel it in their eyes as my dad's shoulders slumped, and my mom avoided looking at me. For them, not wanting to follow the family tradition felt like a rejection—not just of their guidance but of everything they'd worked so hard to build.

The tension was gripping in the following days. My parents never brought it up again, but the sound of silence was more piercing than any argument. I knew they were trying to process what I'd just said and understand why I was so dead-set on doing something different. And I was trying to understand it, too. Well, for all my grit, I still didn't have an answer to their questions. The only thing I knew then was that I could not follow where the path did not feel like mine.

It took a while for me to feel powerful enough to stand by my choice, though I did not have all the answers at that point in time. I started reading about various career paths and options that I had never considered before. It felt overwhelming at first, but it also felt liberating. For the first time in my life, I finally felt as if I had control over my life while disappointing the people whom I cared most about.

Looking back, those conversations with my family were two of the most challenging moments of my life. But, simultaneously, they formed some of the most critical moments. They pushed me to confront fear and stand up for myself in defining what success meant to me, not anyone else. And that was the very first step toward finding your path.

The tension at home has been there for weeks since that dinner conversation. The parents, though hurt by the situation, did not bring up the issue with my future again, at least not openly. Nevertheless, I felt it in my parents' eyes; I heard it in the whispers when they thought I wasn't listening. They just didn't understand why I was so obsessed with staying away from family tradition; I wasn't finger-pointing at them. How could they? Barely did I.

In all this, my grandfather quietly became my unsuspecting ally. One afternoon, as I sat in the living room pretending to read a book, he pulled a chair beside me. His voice, soft but steady, broke the silence. "Bhavik," he said, "I hear you've been giving your parents a hard time."

I was stunned. I had no clue how to say anything. Grandfather wasn't a man who demanded obedience or commanded respect; he was just an older, heavier man whose presence commanded attention. The physician lived a good, long life, respected by everyone who knew him. His words carried with them both wisdom and experience.

"I'm not trying to make a point," I said at last, looking down at the book in my lap. "I just... I don't think I want to be a doctor."

He nodded slowly as if waiting for me to say this. "It's not easy, leaving behind what you're supposed to do. But it's harder to live a life that isn't yours."

I stared at him, aghast. He smiled palely, and the wrinkles around his eyes grew more profound. "I wasn't always convinced that I wanted to be a doctor, you see," he said. But it was then, and we didn't have the freedom you enjoy now. If you're serious about this, you must be courageous enough to tell us that. "

His words felt like a lifeline, something I hadn't even realised I needed. For weeks, I'd been drowning in guilt and uncertainty, but here was someone who understood—someone who wasn't trying to push me into a decision I wasn't ready to make.

My grandfather became a silent ally for the next few weeks. He never tried to persuade my parents to see things from my perspective, but he gave me the strength to hold my ground. When the question of education arose, and my father was unwilling to support my plans, questioning if it was the right choice, my grandfather stood up for me.

"I'll sponsor his education," he said one evening, his voice firm. "It's his life, and he deserves the chance to figure out what he wants to do with it." I will never forget the expression on my father's face during those moments. It was a blend of frustration, resignation, and possibly something like relief. Sitting beside him, my mom quietly nodded in agreement, though she had heavy eyes and was worried. And I knew they weren't on board, but they didn't protest or argue. Grandpa's word was final.

My grandmother was also a tower of strength at that point. My grandfather provided me with the financial support I needed to pursue my business venture, and my grandmother provided something just as invaluable: emotional strength. The quieter of the two always, the one who prefers to sit on the side and just observe, was during that time made her presence felt in subtle ways but meaningfully so.

Every time I felt my family's disappointment weigh upon me, Grandma was there with a gentle word or an encouraging smile. She rarely spoke, but her silent gestures spoke volumes. She came into the room to make me tea when I sat there studying, secretly tucked notes of encouragement into my books, or sat silently beside me when it felt like I could hardly bear the tension in the house.

She walked to where I was sitting on the porch with my eyes lost in the darkness. She sat beside me. In the silence, the clicking of her knitting needles was soothing. Sometime later, she started, "Your parents mean well, Bhavik. They just want you to be happy and safe. However, happiness does not come when you do what others expect from you. Happiness comes when you do the right thing for your heart.

I looked at her with streaming eyes. "What if I fail?" I whispered.

She waited for a moment before responding, "Then you'll have learned, and you'll try again, and at least you will have shown yourself to be brave enough to try."

It stuck in my mind long after that night. Those words were my mantra, reminding me that failure is not the end of everything; it's a part of knowing oneself and where I want to go.

In the following months, I saw little change in my parents. They still worried about my choices, but they also began to trust me, little by little. Though hesitant, my dad started asking about my plans with genuine curiosity instead of frustration. My mom, always the mediator, tried to bridge the gap between us. My grandparents, steadfast in their support, reminded me daily that I wasn't alone.

Looking back, I feel fortunate to have had them in my life. Only some get this kind of support, even when their chosen path takes work. It was never easy, and there were times of doubt and conflict, but it set everything up for the following times. They taught me sometimes that beating expectations wasn't about proving people wrong but demonstrating to oneself that one indeed has the strength and courage to pursue one's dreams.

Chapter 3: The American Dream

While planning to study abroad was not something I had ever dreamed about, it began as an idea that grew slowly yet indeed while I pondered my uncertain future. The thought of leaving behind everything familiar, family, and my lifestyle at home was exciting yet terrifying.[But it felt necessary. I wanted a new beginning, a shot to learn who I was and what I wanted outside of the expectations that defined my life thus far.

I planned my move with secrecy, not because I didn't want everyone to know about it, but because I didn't feel like answering questions and dealing with the doubt that was sure to ensue. I even withheld it from my closest friends. I thought it was fragile, too new, too precious to share. It needed some time to germinate within me before it could endure the examination of others.

Weeks were spent searching for appropriate universities, poring over brochures and websites late into the night. Each school promised something different: freedom, opportunities, a chance to reinvent myself. But simultaneously, the logistics were overwhelming- application forms, entrance exams, essays, deadlines- a maze I had to decipher independently. I couldn't rely on my parents for support at that time; they were just getting over the shock of me not becoming a doctor, and I did not want to heap more of this uncertainty on them.

The biggest challenge was re. Studying abroad wasn't just about academics; it was about living in the unknown, with the comfort of home behind your back and a new beginning in a completely foreign environment. Dreaded failure loomed large against the hope of discovering something else, something better. I clung to that hope like a rope.

I realized just how low I had pitched it. Writing my personal essays was one of the hardest things for me. How do you put all your life down in a few paragraphs? How do you explain what you dream about when you are still unsure what they are? I rewrote those essays more times than I can count, trying to find the balance between honest and aspirational.

Once the applications were submitted, the waiting began. It was a nerve-wracking period, filled with equal parts anticipation and dread. Every email notification made my heart race. When the first acceptance letter came through, I couldn't believe it. I stared at the screen for an eternity, rereading the words repeatedly. I had done it. It felt like the chips had finally started falling in place.

Telling my family was the next big step, and I approached them with mixed feelings. My grandparents were somewhat over the moon, especially my grandfather, who offered me unwavering support. My parents were cautious, though proud of me. They worried about what lay ahead for me. "It's a big step, Bhavik," my dad said, his voice tinged with concern. "Are you sure you're ready for this?"

"I have to try," I replied, and for the first time, I truly believed it. The weeks that followed passed in a blur. There were forms to fill out, documents to gather, and endless checklists to complete. It was too much to handle, especially on the logistical side, but the emotional aspect of leaving home hurt me the most. As the departure date grew closer, reality began to sink in.

I was leaving everything I knew for an entirely uncertain future.

Yet, amid all the chaos and fear, there was this quiet sense of determination. For the first time in a long time, I felt like I was in control of my life. This was my decision, journey, and chance to choose a path.

The daunting task of securing a visa quickly overshadowed the excitement of being accepted into a university in the United States. The visa process would have felt like climbing a mountain if the applications and essays had been overwhelming.

The entire process was anxiety-inducing. The first was accumulating all necessary documents, including financial statements, letters of recommendation, and proof of ties to the home country. It felt like gathering pieces of a confusing puzzle. Every piece had to fit perfectly, and very little could be left to chance. My family shared the tension, though they tried not to show it. My mom fussed over every detail, double-checking my paperwork to make sure nothing was missing. My dad, usually calm and composed, seemed quieter than usual as if the weight of my decision had finally settled on him. Even my grandparents, who had been my biggest supporters, were visibly anxious.

It was as if we were all waiting for the result.

I remember barely sleeping the night before the visa interview. I thought about all the scenarios that might go wrong: "What if I forget some essential thing?" "What if the officer feels I don't want to study seriously?" 'What if they reject me altogether? 'The fear was near paralysing, but at its core was a glimmer of hope—a reminder of why I was doing all this in the first place.

My mom made me breakfast on the interview day, but I couldn't eat because I was too nervous. My dad sat beside me and encouraged me, but he was anxious. "Just be honest," he said. Speak from the heart. They'll see how much this means to you.

Walking into the consulate was like stepping onto a battlefield. The lines were long, and the atmosphere was heavy with anticipation. Everyone around me looked as nervous as I did, holding their documents like lifelines. When my number was called, my heart pounded so loudly that I could barely hear my thoughts.

The interview itself was a blur. The officer asked me questions about my university, my plans, and my family's ability to support me financially. I answered confidently, though my hands shook a little as I passed over my documents. When the officer nodded and said, "Your visa is approved," I felt a wave of relief so powerful that it nearly knocked me over.

I walked out of the consulate clutching my passport, and the burden of the last few weeks finally lifted off my shoulders. Seeing my family waiting for me outside, I couldn't help but grin. "I got it," I squeaked, breaking my voice apart. My mom hugged me tight, tears streaming down her face. My dad clapped me on the back, his pride shining through his usual stoicism. Even my grandparents, who rarely showed their emotions so openly, looked visibly relieved.

The evening back home was quiet. There were no over-the-top celebrations but rather an atmosphere of pride and encouragement. I could finally feel how my family genuinely supported this decision of mine. Of course, they had their fears about it, but their support never wavered.

As I lay in bed that night, thinking about this moment, I realised it was not merely about getting a study visa for a university in the USA. Still, it was also a sign from the Universe that I could achieve my goals with focused efforts. For a long time, I had doubted my ability to step outside of what others expected of me, to take risks, and pursue something entirely different. But now, for the first time, I felt like I was on the right path.

These were the days of relief and newfound doubts. My mom, grandfather, and sister rallied around me, providing unconditional support, but it still seemed my dad did not trust me. He didn't express his displeasure in so many words; on the contrary, it felt like he was repressing his doubts, which were similar to mine.

One evening, as we sat in the living room, my dad finally voiced his concerns. "Bhavik," he said, his tone serious but not unkind, "I want you to succeed, but I'm worried. This is a big step, and there's no guarantee it will work out."

I nodded, understanding his fears. "I know, Dad," I said quietly. "But I have to try. I need to know what I am capable of."
My mom, silently sitting beside us, spoke up then. "He'll make it," she said firmly. "I believe in him, and so should you.

Her confidence was a lifeline for me, a reminder that I wasn't going through this alone. My grandfather, too, remained steadfast in his belief that I was doing the right thing. "It's not about guarantees," he told my dad later. "It's about giving him the chance to find his path.

While busy with her medical career, my sister became a very unexpected source of encouragement. She sent me articles on student life in the US, tips for managing stress, and even links to Indian grocery stores near my university. "You're going to be fine," she said during one of our late-night conversations. "Just stay focused, and don't be afraid to ask for help when you need it."

Their support strengthened me, but at the same time, it put before me a balancing act. Dad's doubts indicated that not everyone had faith in my decision. And I knew how others, from friends and relatives to acquaintances, would criticize it even more. In a society where deviating from the norm was met with scepticism, I was unprepared to face the barrage of questions and opinions that would inevitably arise if people found out about my plans.

So, I kept it to myself and everyone outside my immediate family. It wasn't easy. My friends, who had always been my confidants, asked why I wasn't discussing college applications or entrance exams. "What's your plan, Bhavik?" they'd ask casually, not realising how loaded the question felt to me.

I'd smile and deflect with vague answers about "figuring things out" and "exploring options." It was strange to keep a big part of your life from those you trusted most. But I wasn't ready to share until I knew I could handle the reactions.

It was more complicated to explain to relatives. Indian families, I've learned, are inquisitive ones, and my family is no different. Every phone call seemed to carry similar questions: "Which college Bhavik's going to?

What course is he doing? Have you all thought of his future?" My mom, being the diplomat that she is, would come up with answers that are partially true but not entirely truthful. "We are still deciding," or, "He's shortlisting a couple of them.

As the departure date drew closer, it weighed on me. But still, I knew it was the right decision. I wouldn't want to share my plans too soon, as it would invite doubts and criticism I wasn't ready for.

The day to leave was finally here, and I found it bittersweet and surreal. My friends did not know the whole story, and I had to explain vague reasons for being "busy for a while." My relatives, too, were left with more questions than answers. However, I felt at peace when I hugged my family goodbye at the airport. This was my journey, and I was ready to embrace it wholeheartedly for the first time in my life.

As the plane took off, I peered out of the window into the rapidly shrinking landscape below. My emotions were a mixture of fear, excitement, sadness, and hope. I didn't know what was in store for me, but for the first time, that uncertainty didn't scare me. It felt like freedom.

Chapter 4: Cultural Adaptations

Stepping into the United States for the first time was like landing on another planet. Everything appeared different: the streets, air, people, and how they spoke. Little did I expect the mundane everyday things to turn into a challenge? The first shock came during my orientation at the university. I was dressed in what I considered appropriate "academic attire": a shirt, trousers, and clean shoes. At home, that's the way you dress in the academy. But in this auditorium, I realized I was overdressed. Almost everyone around me wore jeans, shorts, or sweatpants, sporting a baseball cap tilted to one side and sometimes pulling his hood over his face. For a moment, I thought I had entered the wrong auditorium.

I was in for another rude shock in class that day. A middle-aged man with a benevolent smile addressed us and said, "Hi, everyone. I am Tom."

I blinked, wondering if he said that. In India, professors are addressed by title—Dr., Professor, Sir, or Ma'am. This is a sign of respect, and using the first name seems disrespectful.

For the first couple of weeks, I couldn't do it. I avoided addressing professors directly; I just raised my hand or nodded silently. Eventually, however, I understood this informality had nothing to do with disrespect but rather with creating an approachable and relaxed environment.

Even the way students communicated with professors was different. Back home, asking too many questions was sometimes considered disruptive, but here, it was encouraged. The students would interrupt a lecture to clarify a point, disagree with an idea, or share an opinion. I wondered if they were not worried about offending the professor. But watching how the interactions unfolded helped me realize it wasn't about disrespect but curiosity and collaboration.

Another surprising aspect was the group work. In Indian educational systems, group activities are generally characterized by one or two people picking up the slack with minimal contribution from others. At this institution, however, everybody had a share to care for. Each one had a piece of work to do. It was astonishing to see just how serious everyone was about their share of responsibility. They wished to excel rather than simply complete the project.

Even outside of class, I found myself navigating unfamiliar territory. The first thing that struck me was how friendly strangers are. People would smile at me on the street, hold doors open, or say "hi" in passing. I didn't know how to react. Am I supposed to smile back? Say something? In my hometown, people usually only greeted strangers if they had a reason to. It took me a while to realize that these gestures aren't invitations to conversation—just small acts of kindness.

Meals were another adjustment. I was introduced to a new food world in the dining hall—burgers, fries, pizza, and endless sauces and condiments. But what struck me most wasn't the food itself; it was how casually people ate. Students would carry their food and sit wherever they could find space, eating on their laps or walking around. Meals back home were always a ritualistic affair; the family sat at the table and ate. Here, food was merely a fuel for survival, something to fill a busy schedule.

Of course, there were times when the differences seemed too great. I often felt a strong urge to go home during the first few weeks. I missed the order and predictability of life in India, the unspoken rules I had grown up with.

At the same time, I was fascinated by the freedom and openness of this new culture. It was a lot to take in, but I was determined to adapt.

Every day brought something new—something unexpected, something challenging. Though it wasn't always easy, I realized these culture shocks were essential to my journey. They forced me to step outside my comfort zone, question my assumptions, and embrace the unfamiliar. In doing so, I started to see the world—and myself—differently.

I eventually realized that adapting to the US academic system would be gradual. Still, nothing could save me from the rollercoaster of emotions leading up to my first business calculus test. I had always been one of the better math students in college, and though the lecture was challenging, I was optimistic about my chance of passing that examination. I had studied practiced, and was sure I had done enough to pass—maybe not with flying colors, but enough to hold my head high.

I breathed deeply as the results arrived a week later, and the professor delivered my paper. My heart skipped a beat when it showed a 30% top at the beginning. I would pass. In school back home, sometimes passing a test meant nothing, but for me, since I would not have to retake it and since failing one in a foreign culture is somewhat tricky to explain at home, I was simply relieved.

By this point, I had already left the classroom, a faint smile spreading. This wasn't going to be as impossible as I thought. Even though I was finding it hard to get accustomed to the frequent assignments and the competitive atmosphere, if I could pass the first test, I could handle it all.

That afternoon, I sat in the library with a few classmates to review the test. They were flipping through their graded papers, discussing where they had lost points and how to improve for the next exam. When I mentioned my score, one of them raised an eyebrow. "You got 30%?" he asked, with a hint of confusion.

Yes, but it could be better. But at least I passed."

There was an awkward silence before another classmate spoke up: "Uh, Bhavik. The passing grade is 70% here.'

For a moment, I thought they were joking. Indeed, they didn't mean 70%. Back home, a passing grade was usually much lower, often around 30-40%. But as I looked around the table, their expressions confirmed it. My stomach sank. What I thought was a narrow victory was an apparent failure.

Later, I approached my professor to confirm what I had just learned. He greeted me with a kind but knowing smile, as if he'd been waiting for this conversation. "Yes, Bhavik," he said gently. In this class and most others, the passing grade is 70%. I know it's a big adjustment, but you'll get there. Let's talk about how we can improve you for the next test.

I left his office feeling a mix of embarrassment and determination. Realizing I had failed was humbling, but it was also a wake-up call. The academic standards here were higher and stricter, and I couldn't approach my studies like I had back home if I wanted to succeed.

For the next couple of days, I wrestled with self-doubt. Was I cut out for this? Had I made a mistake coming here? But as the initial sting of failure faded, I began to see the situation differently. This wasn't the end—it was an opportunity to learn and grow. I decided to try a little more complicated, not just to pass but to prove that I could rise to the challenge.

I began attending tutoring, something I had never done before. Initially, I felt lost, surrounded by students who appeared much more confident and capable than I was. However, as the weeks went by, I started noticing little things: concepts that seemed confusing before started making sense. I also formed a study group with a few classmates; their support made a huge difference. We'd meet in the library, reviewing practice problems and quizzing each other on key concepts.

When the next test came, I walked into the classroom confident and focused. I didn't know if I would ace it, but I could tell I had worked towards it. When the results came out, I had scored 72%. It wasn't perfect, but it did give me a sense of achievement.

From that came one of the greatest lessons I have ever learned on this journey: failure isn't the opposite of success—it is a stepping stone. It pushes you to work harder, think differently, and grow in ways you never thought were possible. I often used to tell myself this- each setback is yet another step toward becoming the person you were destined to be.

It was not merely an adjustment to academics or the culture but learning how to survive without the comforts of home. It was an overwhelming distance for someone who had never stayed away from family for more than a few days. I missed the warmth of home-cooked meals, the familiar rhythms of my city, and the unspoken understanding of a shared culture. There were days when homesickness suddenly hit like a wave. Yet, in those exact moments, I realized how lucky I was to have family who never let me feel lonely. My family and loved ones were there for me despite being thousands of miles away. My mother called me almost daily to talk about little things—what she had cooked for lunch, updates from relatives, or the latest goings on at home. Her voice was a lifeline, reminding me I was connected to my roots halfway worldwide.

My sister, one of my biggest champions, sent me care packages with things she knew I would miss. From Indian snacks to handwritten notes of encouragement, each package was a piece of home in a box. I would sit in my dorm room, savoring the familiar flavors and reading her letters, and for a little while, the distance didn't seem so daunting.

My grandfather also played a quiet, steady role in keeping me grounded. He did not call as often, but his words were loaded with meaning when he did. "You are doing something brave, Bhavik," he said once on the telephone. Remember, it's not meant to be easy. The challenges and the way you overcome them will help you grow."

While my family's support was invaluable, I also found comfort in the friendships I began to build on campus. At first, I was hesitant to open up to anyone. The cultural differences made me feel like an outsider, and I worried that I wouldn't be able to connect with people. But as the weeks went on, I started to find my footing.

One of my first close friends was Raj, an international student with similar struggles. We bonded over homesickness—long calls with family, the search for good Indian food, and the longing to celebrate seemingly insignificant festivals here. On particularly tough days, we'd cook simple meals together in the communal kitchen, the aroma of spices filling the air and bringing back memories of home.

Another unexpected source of support came from my roommate, Jake. Jake had grown up in the U.S. and was more than happy to introduce me to American customs and culture. He taught me to love Sunday football games and how they were played over slices of pizza in the dorm. "You're one of us now," he joked one day, handing me a team jersey. It was a small gesture but it made me feel like I belonged.

At midnight, I had conversations with my friends. We shared moments of vulnerability, talking about our families, fears, and dreams. In those moments, I realized I was not alone in my homesickness. Everyone, in their own way, felt something was missing. For some, it was the childhood home; for others, it was the certainty of a life that had been left behind. Those conversations became a source of strength, reminding us we were all together.

What struck me most about those early months in the USA were the random acts of kindness from people who were so diverse from me. Whether it was a classmate willing to review the notes with me, a professor explaining a difficult concept, or a friend inviting me to join them for Thanksgiving dinner, I was surrounded by kindness in ways I hadn't anticipated. It didn't make the homesickness disappear but made it easier to bear.

As time passed, I learned to balance my identity between who I was brought up as and the new experiences that were now molding my worldview. I started finding solace in the simple stuff, like discovering an Indian grocery store an hour away and stockpiling spices and snacks. I even joined a campus cultural group celebrating Diwali with music and food, bringing home to the university. I even went as far as sharing fragments of my culture with my friends by introducing them to

Bollywood films and teaching them how to brew chai. There was some satisfaction in that no matter how far off I was, I could still wear my identity as a badge.

Those early months were some of my life's most challenging yet transformative moments. Not only did I see a change in my relationship with academics, but I also realized the importance of kinship and a sense of belonging. Through my family's unwavering faith and the friendships I built, I learned that home isn't just a place. The people remind you of who you are no matter where you go.

Chapter 5: Building a Support Network

One of the key takeaways from my time in the USA was that the bonds that I share with the people in my surroundings would significantly impact my lifestyle. With my childhood buddies back home, the understanding that I shared was a byproduct of similar cultural backgrounds. But here, in this faraway land, everything would start all over again for me, and so many alien faces around me had made it feel a little daunting.

The first few weeks were the hardest. Often, I ate alone, walked alone, and studied alone. It was not that people were unfriendly; on the contrary, their friendliness initially felt a little intimidating to me. Everyone else seemed to be adjusting effortlessly, forming friendships and making plans while I drifted on the edges, unsure how to fit in.

Only after failing my first test in Business Calculus did I begin to understand the importance of having a support system. Loneliness hit me like a wave, and I realized it was high time I stepped out of my comfort zone.

. It wasn't easy at first. Introducing myself to strangers in class or at campus events felt awkward, and I constantly worried about saying the wrong thing. But I continued, hoping that one real connection would make a difference.

My first success occurred in the library during a study session. I joined a small group of students from my Business Calculus class, all reviewing material for a quiz. Ethan was one of them. I found him laid-back, easy-going, and adept at simplifying complex concepts. After the session, he began talking to me, asking where I was from and how I was doing on campus.

However, the way Etan approached people was appealing. He didn't ask questions out of politeness- he seemed genuinely interested. As we sat there talking, I talked to him about stuff that I had not shared with anyone since moving to the States. I told him about my loneliness, my irritation with the college system, and even the cultural differences that made me uncomfortable. To my surprise, he did not downplay my feelings at all. Instead, he listened intently and then shared some of the challenges from his first year in college.

That conversation marked the beginning of a deep and long-lasting friendship. Ethan had a way of adding humor and a clear perspective to the most stressful situations. He introduced me to his circle of friends—a mix of international students and locals—and encouraged me to join them for everything, from late-night study sessions to spontaneous trips to the nearest diner.

Ethan introduced me to Raj, another international student. Little did I anticipate that he would become one of my closest confidants and someone I could count on.

As my circle of friends increased, so did my confidence. I began to feel included on and off campus. With my new friends, I found the confidence to try new things: watching my first football game, joining a cultural club, or even approaching a stranger and conversing. These little steps made me feel slightly more comfortable in this place that felt so foreign.

It was surprising how warm and pleasant the people I encountered during those early months were. My American roommate, Jake, quietly explained football rules and invited me to spend Thanksgiving at his house. My classmate Maria checked in after every exam to see how it had gone. Countless others offered advice, shared their stories, or simply made me feel seen and heard.

Looking back, I realize how much these friendships shaped my experience. They weren't just about having people to spend time with; they were more about the joy of shared camaraderie. Living far away from home started to feel less challenging. f.

After a few weeks on campus, I realized that if one wishes to thrive in a new environment, he cannot wait for connections to happen. He has to reach out to people actively. For a person like me, this is easier said than done. However, loneliness was a strong motivator, especially during the early days. I knew I needed to take that first awkward step if I was to find my way.

I started small by interacting with my classmates during lectures. I sat where the same group sat each time for every lecture session, hoping the familiarity would blossom. After each class, we discussed the subjects, asked for clarifications on specific topics, and shared our thoughts.

Maria was one of my first friends, always carrying a notebook full of notes. One afternoon, I asked if I could borrow her notes to review something I had missed in class. She agreed, but not just that; she offered to study with me for the quiz. Maria's attitude inspired me, and I became proactive in my search for friends.

Also, outside the classrooms, I attended campus events, even those that did not initially attract me. One evening, I walked into a trivia night at the student union, lured by free pizza. I didn't know anyone there but joined a team anyway, introducing myself with a nervous smile. By the end of that night, I had learned more about obscure history in the United States than I ever cared to learn, and I exchanged contact information with two teammates who would later become my inner circle.

Another critical moment was when I joined an international student group on campus. This organization had regular weekly meetups, where students from around the world met and shared their experiences and lives with one another. It is where I got to know Priya, another Indian student who was a semester ahead of me. She quickly became this mentor, dispensing practical advice on everything- from where to get cheap groceries to how to negotiate the bureaucracy of student services. Her guidance greatly aided in getting things done, but her friendship reminded me that I was not alone.

As I became more confident and reached out, I began to find connections everywhere: I'd talk to whoever was behind me in line at the cafeteria and join informal pickup soccer games at the quad. I even approached people randomly in the library when they seemed free. One evening, waiting in line for coffee at a university café, I started talking with Alex, only to discover we were in the same class. That chance meeting resulted in a study group that improved my grades and helped me network with some supportive peers.

The most difficult shift for me was turning every contact into an opportunity for connection since friendships develop back home over time and, to a great extent, are anchored to the history and circumstances they have in common. Here, I learned that genuine relationships demand conscious effort. It wasn't a matter of waiting for the right people to cross my path, but instead, a matter of proactivity- to initiate an introduction, ask questions, and take an interest in other people's lives. It also helped me realize the importance of vulnerability: I told them how homesick I felt during dinner one evening with new acquaintances. I was not finding it easy to settle into life there. I was shocked when almost everyone at the table nodded in understanding. Those from the U.S. said they had felt homesick or overwhelmed sometimes. That conversation reminded me that everyone has struggles, no matter where they're from—and that sharing them can bring people closer together.

By the end of that semester, I had cultivated a network of friends and acquaintances who enriched my life in many ways. They were not some random strangers that I hung out with. For me, they became and remained a support system, a source of comfort and encouragement during the challenges of moving to a different place. As I went on to create those ties and connections, I became different in ways I never thought I could be. I became more self-assured and bold. I became open to new connections and academic opportunities by letting go of shyness.

Looking back, I realize that reaching out isn't only about finding people to lean on and developing emotional resilience. Every talk, every new friendship, brought me closer to a life that would be worthwhile and complete, regardless of where I was. In the process, I found that the best way to find a connection is to offer it: showing up for people, listening, and sharing your thoughts with them.

Food was one of the most challenging parts of living in a foreign land. The food back home was rich in flavor and was prepared with warm, loving hands. Here, every meal was a reminder of how far I was from that. My first few attempts at cooking Indian dishes in the dorm kitchen ended in disasters of overcooked rice, missing spices, and more frustration than flavor. Nevertheless, those meals became a part of holding onto my roots.: Raj provided information on an Indian grocery store within about an hour's travel from home.

Entering the aisles of the Indian store became reminiscent of my childhood: basmati rice, garam masala, turmeric, and packets of Maggi noodles brought back memories of midnight snacks. That evening, we turned the dorm kitchen into a small Indian restaurant, made khichdi, and discussed whether the amount of salt was too much. The smells filled the hallway, and students from other classes asked what smelled so good. Soon, I was experimenting with the food on campus. The cafeteria meals became the canvas for creativity: rice and beans got a dash of f cumin, and sandwiches, without much thought, even on plain bread, were livened with a pinch of chaat masala that I carried. None of the fast food joints that I relished served orange chicken. It was not Indian, but something about that tangy, sweet, and spicy taste was reminiscent of the Indo-Chinese dishes we had in college.

We funnily renamed it "the campus chicken Manchurian," a food that became a comfort during those long study sessions. As my culinary skills improved, I invited more friends to eat Indian food. Watching them relish utter chicken, biryani, or paneer tikka filled me with pride and a way to connect with my roots while sharing a piece of myself with them. Watching Ethan struggle to say "jeera rice" or Maria's eyes widen at a mouthful of spicy curry was funny. And as per convention, food became a wholesome way of bonding with strangers. Then, my friends introduced me to their comfort food. Jake taught me how to love Southern biscuits and gravy; Maria taught me how to make tamales.

Each new meal has stories to be shared and memories to be made. The kitchen, dining table, and experiments brought a sense of familiarity to unfamiliar surroundings. The aroma of familiar spices and the comfort of familiar tastes strengthened my bond with my heritage.

With every meal, I merged my old and new worlds, creating a sense of belonging in something that had once seemed like a far-fetched dream.

Chapter 6: Suggestions for Life Abroad

Everything seemed new: the language, the culture, the people, and even the air. It was like stepping into a movie without knowing what I auditioned for. It was all vibrant, fast, and too much. I did not take long to realize that, to make it in this new world, I had to let go of everything I assumed I was supposed to be and become open-minded towards everything.

My first lesson came during one of the first group projects in Business Calculus class. With group projects back home, in most cases, one or two students would do all the work while everyone else coasted along. So, I had assumed the same in this case, so I prepared myself to take on most of the load. But as we divided assignments, I was surprised to see how seriously everyone took their work. My classmates came from Brazil, South Korea, and the U.S., among many other places, but approached this project with a remarkable sense of teamwork. They had ideas and listened to one another, which was foreign to me; it was not about hierarchy or disagreement but collaboration. This newfound appreciation of what diversity truly brings has helped me not only in my grades but also in developing a better perspective on my life.

I also had to learn communication methods in ways I'd never done before. For example, I was surprised by people's casual attitudes reflected in their words. Professors wanted to be called by their first names; people would smile, greet me warmly while passing by on the streets, and voice opinions in classes without compunction. Frankly speaking, such behavior would have seemed borderline rude back home, yet I found it commonplace here. I could not participate due to the fear of saying the wrong things. I was afraid of being offensive without knowing. However, I learned that people were not looking for perfectionism and asked me to present myself before them and try. Just a simple "thank you": if someone held the door or commented on the weather as it was, it could get you to start connecting with others.

My first potluck dinner is memorable. Many guys from my dorm invited me; I had no idea what it would be. We had home-cooked food when we ate and usually ate as a family. This reminded me of home. So I wanted to make something easy: dal and rice. But, what if they hated it? What if it was not good enough? When I went there, however, everybody greeted me warmly, asking me what I had brought. Friends welcomed me by introducing their dishes: lasagna, tacos, dumplings, and what seemed to be a "family recipe" casserole. It was warm and inviting; before I knew it, the night had gone, and I knew I'd not only dined but had a homely experience.

I had to unlearn some preconceptions as I adapted to local customs. For instance, I had never considered small talk meaningful or worthwhile. In my background, people tend to be straightforward and to the point; hence, I had never really considered the art of casual chit-chat. I learned to appreciate people at the bus stop, in the line at the cafeteria, and even the cashier when buying groceries. It was awkward initially, but I began to see it as a good way to connect people in small ways. Now, all this small talk was also a little moment of human connection, brightening my day and reminding me how easy it is to be kind with the most trivial gestures.

All this, I learned while living abroad, was not merely adapting oneself to another environment but learning to embrace the lifestyle. It means letting go of your rigid perspectives, listening to others' stories about their experiences, questioning theirs without a fearful judgment, or finding pleasure in the unfamiliar.

One thing I'd tell someone leaving to live in another country for the first time is to be curious, respect each circumstance, and listen to every person you can. If you don't get something, just ask. More often than not, people enjoy sharing their culture with others if they seem sincere. If something feels awkward or uncomfortable, pull back a step and try looking at it through another lens. When you are wrong, which happens, and it's something that you laugh about and take lessons from because living abroad is like a trip of constant discoveries, not only outside but also with yourself. And it pushes you in ways you cannot even imagine and makes you find friendships in places you never saw yourself.

Looking back, I realize that keeping my mind open was essential for everything. That is how I became friends with people from many different places in the world, adapted to a vastly different culture, and finally gained a sense of belonging in a place once so foreign to me. It also taught me that the world is much more significant and beautiful than I would have thought.

One of the first lessons I learned about living abroad was that it's not the grand achievements that make you feel at home in a new place—it's the little victories, the small moments of joy that sneak up on you when you least expect them. I did not find many chances to think about those minute things in the initial few months because there were so many considerable things to absorb- culture shock, academic rigor, and this new space. However, it later formed my lifeline here, holding me together in this lavish, massive city.

One incident etched into my mind: I was traveling alone on public transport. While still a few blocks from home, at least I wasn't worrying over buses or trains; everything was familiar, and I knew by heart the best routes. Well, here was the new city that was unfamiliar to me; even deciphering which bus line to take sounded like solving some sort of puzzle. One afternoon, I set out, armed with Google Maps and a healthy dose of nervous energy to explore this café that I had read about online. Not too far of a distance, but the nervousness of getting the wrong bus or missing my stop made my stomach flip. The pride of getting off at the right stop was even better than expected. What it was worth in itself—the good lighting in a friendly café, the decent barista—seemed pretty diminutive next to the feeling of independence that had been won.

Moments started to pile up: the first time I encountered a gorgeous hidden park nestled among quiet residential homes, the first time I survived an entire conversation with a stranger without making mistakes with words, and the first time I cooked a simple Indian meal that tasted like home. Each of these small victories was mine—almost insignificant in the grand scheme of things, but mine. They reminded me that I could adapt and find beauty and comfort in a place that had once felt foreign.

Cooking became a source of both joy and accomplishment. Initially, I burned rice, made watery curries, and made hundreds of unsuccessful attempts. With each failure, I learned something, and the day I finally made the proper dal and rice, waves of satisfaction sprang up unexpectedly. It wasn't about the food; it was about the connection to home, the sense of agency, and realizing that I could take care of myself.

These small moments also helped with homesickness. If I felt a hollow feeling for missing my family or the comforts of home, I would begin focusing on what I had instead of all that I had lost. I learned to find pleasure in the ordinary, and the ordinary turns into magnificent. Starting with crisp autumn air during a walk to class, the kind act of a stranger who opens the door, or a feeling of accomplishment after finishing an assignment, these simple pleasures did not take away the hustle, but there was a reason to continue.

Looking back, I realize that only these tiny victories make life abroad meaningful. They remind me that growth does not happen overnight. Still, each takes you closer to yourself in small, incremental steps.

It meant finding a little joy in small things or pushing past fear; it meant challenging myself to grow. And somehow, living abroad made me face the fears I did not even know existed—the fear of failure, rejection, and, above all, of leaving my comfort zone. These came in big and small ways for me, and every test was a test of my will to adapt.

Joining a student club was one of my earliest challenges. I had never signed up for extracurricular activities back home. I used to keep myself within my small circle of friends and avoid all unnecessary social situations. Here, I did not have that luxury. I had to put myself out there if I wanted to make connections. One afternoon, I was walking by a table on campus where an advertisement was placed for a cultural club. They hosted an event later that week, and the student at the booth was urging me to come. Not knowing whether I'd fit into the group or if people would be interested in talking with me made the thought slightly daunting, but something told me to push through.

It was pretty nerve-wracking going into that event. I didn't know anyone inside, and for the first few minutes, I lingered near the back of the room, doing my best to appear busy on my phone. But as the night wore on, I made myself talk to the person sitting next to me. To my surprise, they were warm and welcoming, and by the end of the evening, I had exchanged numbers with a few new acquaintances. It was a small step, but it felt monumental at the time. It reminded me that fear loses its power when you face it head-on.

The second fear I had to overcome was that of asking for help. Sometimes, asking questions back home could feel like an admission of weakness. This is also my mindset when coming to the U.S. Of course, it wasn't too long before I realized that only so much can be done individually. At every point of need, whether asking a professor to explain some unclear concept or seeking advice from a senior student regarding course selection, I found people more than willing to help me. It was not about being weak but about making connections and learning.

What I feared most was failing. I have always feared making mistakes or disappointing people, but life outside the country has taught me that failure is not a destination but part of the journey. Losing my way back from college, messing up my speaking words, or even getting bad marks on some assignments taught me to accept and grow from all experiences. I started slowly to let go of fear, thinking that I was not a failure; sometimes, the most significant step you'd take would have to do with failure to attain success.

If I learned something from fear, it has a way of telling you that you are near some growth. At those times, I was in fear, such as introducing myself to new people, trying something new, or admitting that I did not know everything, which made me stronger, more confident, and open to possibilities in life. And with facing my fears came the realization of how much more I could do than I had imagined.

Leaving home for the first time is a strange combination of excitement, anxiety, and doubt. In the weeks leading up to my departure, my emotions felt on a constant loop, alternating between anticipation and fear. One moment, I'd feel exhilarated at the thought of starting a new life in the United States, imagining all the opportunities ahead. The second is I'd feel the weight of leaving behind family, friends, and the comfort of familiarity.

The excitement was easy to cling to. One would dream about independence, new people, and adventures waiting to be had. But anxiety crept in in quieter moments: What if I couldn't hack it? What if I was a misfit? What if this decision turned out to be a mistake? These doubts weren't loud or dramatic; they were subtle, like a persistent whisper in the back of my mind.

One of the hardest things about preparing to leave was saying goodbye to my family. My parents tried to stay strong, but I could see the worry in their eyes. My mom hugged me tighter each day while my dad gave me practical advice about money, travel, and safety. My grandparents are proud of me, but mixed with that was sadness. "You're brave," my grandfather told me one evening, "but it doesn't mean you won't feel fear. It means you'll face it anyway.

Building up my support system in my mind helped prepare me for this transition. I was there as much as possible for my family and was making as much time for my loved ones as possible to cherish moments I would later miss. I was in contact with other friends who had spent a term abroad to learn about what they would face, but the challenges are worthwhile, I realized from their stories.

Something that stayed in my mind was to be mindful of your goal and focus. Those farewells seemed pretty heavy, yet having our eyes fixated on the larger goal helped us concentrate and return to reality.
I started journaling, too, while on this adventure. Getting all that stuff out sometimes really helped my mind develop in the sense I was thinking; on more challenging days, of course, I put on paper what I was looking forward to, or what I was hoping to pull from it all and why exactly I made such a choice anyway.

Far from a pro, five minutes of attention on my breath was enough to calm the tornado within my brain. It reminded me that it's perfectly fine to be overwhelmed sometimes and that one didn't have it all figured out right then.
I was highly reliant on my family and closest friends at that time. Their support kept me going, and they brought me back down to earth when my emotions tended to spin out of control. Mom's reassuring words, Dad's practical wisdom, and my sister's humor reminded me of one truth I had never forgotten: I wasn't alone, no matter where I went.

On the day of my departure, I was all nervous. However, once I boarded the plane, I could see the last lights of my city at the other end of the windowpane. At that moment, this calmness engulfed me. It was not that I was leaving alone; I was beginning something new.

I learned so many lessons that no classroom could ever teach. It made me grow up overnight, take full responsibility for myself, and navigate a world in which every single decision was made by me and me alone. At first, that was terrifying; I had to figure everything out independently. Back home, I would always have a family to call upon for some advice, support, or a home-cooked meal.

The first time I felt I had changed was when I had to deal with a minor crisis myself. In the middle of winter, my heater stopped working in my apartment, and since I had never been exposed to freezing temperatures, I was unprepared for this situation. My first reaction was to freak out and call my dad, but then I stopped myself. I looked for local repair services, contacted the landlord, and was able to get it sorted out in a day. It wasn't a significant achievement, but reminded me that I could handle my problems without someone else's intervention.

The next big feat in my life was financial independence. Controlling expenses while aboard was a lesson in discipline. Here, I learned to budget, check the expenditures that occurred, and decide what to compromise on and what not to consider within my expenses. There are days when one would even forget about not worrying about these things, but the control over one's things and self-sufficiency are valuable.

I became more confident in making significant and little decisions independently, without second-guessing myself. Whether it was choosing a major, where to spend my weekends, or even what steps to take after graduation, I began to rely on my instincts and choose my path.

It's not really about the practical skills; it's about my mindset. Living abroad taught me how to be resilient and adaptable and to keep a mind open to new experiences, taking failure not as something to be feared but as something to be learned from, that independence does not only mean doing everything alone but knowing when it's time to seek help and when it's time to stand on one's own two feet.

I look back and can see how much I changed in those years. I came in as someone who did not know himself and was unwilling to step out of his comfort zone. I left as a person who is confident and self-reliant and who dares to face challenges that lay ahead. Living abroad wasn't just an adventure; it was a transformation in the aspects of a person toward his future.

Chapter 7: Redefining Success

As I grew older, I thought success was measured by one thing: money. It wasn't about happiness, growth, or the richness of experiences—it was about how much one earned. I had seen this around me, in how people talked about someone who had "made it," like their worth was directly measured by the car they drove or where they lived. It wasn't a personal belief but an internalized philosophy that culture, family, and surroundings had shaped.

In my family, success has always been equated with professional achievements. Wealth was a byproduct of higher education and respectable professional ventures. My grandfather was a highly respected physician. I looked up to him because of the richness he obtained through the gratitude and respect his patients gave him. However, my parents had a different viewpoint, wherein they thought that monetary advancement leads to immense personal freedoms. Conversations at home often revolved around whether someone's career was progressing as expected and how much a person earned in a particular year. Hence, the implicit reminder was that money wasn't needed—it was required.

Hence, my teenage dreams were shaped by the desire to make a quick buck, regardless of career or profession. I was fascinated by stories of entrepreneurs who built empires from scratch and investment bankers who earned millions in a single night, mainly to figure out how they had earned that money. Success, to me, was all about numbers. The bigger the number in your bank account, the more successful you were.

I envied those respected simply because of their wealth, yet I secretly desired the same. I wanted to spend money without any second thought, and my mind constantly thought of ways to earn societal approval through my monetary status. I knew these beliefs would be tested the minute I moved abroad.

My first taste of financial success was during my teenage. A family friend immediately taught me about trading and the stock market, and I was hooked. It felt like an excellent way to make money by investing in stocks and watching their value soar. Initially, I placed a small wager with someone's help, and soon enough, I earned a paltry profit. To my pubescent self, I felt like I had the potential to make a lot of money from the comfort of my home, and that too with minimal effort. I read everything about market trends, which stocks to invest in, and the best time to invest, and I did so with a manic dedication. I envisioned my future life where I would be rich even before graduation and never worry about career prospects or finding a job because money would never be a problem.

The cracks in my definition of success began to appear within the first few months of being overseas. I was still in love with the notion that money was the means and the end. However, as soon as I met people from different backgrounds with varying definitions of success, my perceptions shifted.

The first thing that hit me was the American work culture. In India, missing meals, working through the weekend,d and working long hours are prided upon. .. The more hours you worked, the more successful you were. In America, however, I witnessed individuals who took the extra effort to have a life beyond the workplace and cherished personal time and work. Professors and students also had different frames of mind—success was not just about climbing the corporate ladder but also about personal satisfaction, making space for hobbies and relationships, and maintaining good mental health.

One night, I stayed up and chatted with my professor, Dr. Mitchell. He had defected from finance into academia. He did not impulsively give up a lucrative corporate job on impulse. It was the complete opposite of anything that I was ever taught to believe. I questioned why he left, and his explanation made me question my perception of wealth.

"You can earn only money up to a certain point in life," he replied, leaning back in his chair. "I was making more money than I could spend and was miserable. I was working 80-hour weeks, never seeing my family, living in a state of stress. I asked myself, is this the way I want to live?'?"

I didn't know what to say. I had never seen anybody deliberately prefer happiness to economic progress. But Dr. Mitchell was not the only one. Gradually, I encountered more and more individuals—colleagues, professionals, even strangers-who did not consider material wealth to be the yardstick by which personal success is measured. Some took up work they were passionate about, even if it was slightly less remunerative. Others preferred traveling, learning, or art over money. Their happiness stemmed from internal fulfillment, not from mere bank notes.

It took me much time to wrap my head around this thought process. Why would a person take a less-paying job f when they can push themselves to earn more? Why would someone spend time doing something that had no economic profits?? But over time, observing these people, I saw something else—these individuals were happy in a way I had never seen before. They weren't always chasing the next material thing or a specific figure in their bank account. They found indulging in their passions and personal goals more lucrative than earning more money.

One of the experiences that sticks in my memory is meeting an exchange student from whom I learned that I studied environmental studies and aimed to work for an NGO upon graduation. He laughed when I asked him if he was concerned about making a living.

"I don't need much," he answered. "Provided I'm useful and can travel occasionally, I'm happy."

That exchange has stayed with me. He was not seeking success—he was living on his terms.

These things made me question my values. Did I want to spend my life working to make money for money's sake? Would I be happier and more prosperous if I had been taught to think so? The more I considered these questions, the more I understood that the definition of success is individualistic, and perhaps it was time to alter my definition.

Living overseas was a humbling experience in ways I had never anticipated. Back home, I thought that talent, brains, and economic prosperity were the formulas for success. But in America, I discovered that talent would not do; resilience was the key to success. Every obstacle, every failure, and every moment of uncertainty helped me let go of my preconceived notions and redefine what success is.

One of my initial major disappointments was academics. Although optimistic, I struggled in some classes, including Business Calculus. The grading, the workload, and the professors' encouragement of self-learning made it impossible for me to succeed. There was no hand-holding, no acceptance of late work, and no shortcuts to catch up once you were behind. When I failed my first midterm, I was filled with self-doubt. Was I even qualified to do this? Had I made a massive mistake in attending here?

Financial difficulties were another source of stress. Despite my planning before leaving the country, unexpected expenses—higher rent than I expected, expensive textbooks, and daily costs—started to deplete my savings at an alarming pace. It bothered me to ask my parents for money. Being financially independent meant a lot, and having to ask for help seemed like failure.

For a while, I let these obstacles get the better of me. I questioned whether I was clever and hard-working enough to make it. But then something shifted. I realized I had two choices: I could mope around it, or I could fight through it.

I started implementing small but sustainable changes. I created study groups for my most challenging courses, spending hours studying with struggling students. I attended my professor's office hours and questioned them, which I initially found embarrassing but ultimately beneficial. I also worked a part-time job on campus. It didn't pay very well—it was just a library shift—but it relieved some of my financial pressure.

One of the memorable challenges I faced was being assigned as the group leader for a project in one of my business classes. Public speaking and leadership were not my forte, but I had no option but to comply. Our group had issues. We were way behind deadlines, and there was no leadership, so I promised myself that we wouldn't fail. I challenged myself to speak louder, keep our priorities in order, and ensure everyone shared the burden. When we finally turned in our project, not only did we get one of the best grades in class, but my professor took me aside and said, "You're a natural leader, Bhavik."

It moved something within. It wasn't mere intelligence that had gotten through; it was perseverance. That understanding marked the start of my personal development, compelling me to confront my fears instead of running away from them.

As I settled further into my new life, my definition of success changed. If determination had made me resilient, personal growth had shown me what was necessary. I had spent years pursuing external validation, such as grades, money, and compliments, but now, I began to look within.

For the first time, I began to invest in experiences and not solely materialistic things. I started looking beyond academics, reading books that challenged my worldview and broadened my perspective. I began to travel more, to ties close to home, and appreciated the journey as much as possible. I learned new things, some practical, such as budgeting and time management, and others simply for pleasure, such as photography and writing.

Volunteering at a homeless shelter left a profound impact on my psyche. My friends had invited me to go with them, and I wasn't even sure that was something I could do. But something changed within me when I began serving meals to individuals who had less than I'd ever had. It was not about how much money or power I acquired but what I could give back to the world. The feeling of fulfillment that I experienced in that moment outweighed any kind of monetary reward that I ever received.

One night, while sitting in the park with my friends, watching the sunset after a challenging and draining semester, I suddenly realized something. At that particular moment, I wasn't concerned with grades, finances, or my career. I was simply... happy. It had always seemed to me, all those years, that happiness was the result of a successful life, but it suddenly occurred to me that happiness was the success for which I'd been striving the entire time.

This change in thinking did not involve being any less ambitious or working less.. It just meant that I no longer measured myself by my bank balance. I began measuring success by growth, experience, and peace of mind instead of validation from others.

By the last phase of my schooling, I was a different person. I still prized success, but not at the cost of my well-being. I still desired to be financially stable, but not at the expense of my happiness. I still wanted to win, both in my endeavors and my career.

That was the biggest lesson I learned living overseas: success is about reaching the top and being the best version of yourself.

Reflecting on who came to America initially, I was obsessed with numbers, status, and financial validation. ., . When I was a kid, success had a simple meaning-amassing large amounts of wealth. But the definition changed drastically as I grew up. Overseas, life shattered the foundations of my former thinking and molded them afresh. Through loss and triumph, solitude and love, and doubting everything I had ever known, I realized that success changed me for the remainder of my life: success is not about what you gain but rather about who you become.

.

I chased titles, money, and security in my early years because I believed these would be enough for me. However, I now seek purpose, passion, and influence—none money can purchase. I no longer chase the illusion that I will be happy if I can make some money or get a career rank. Instead, I should focus on what truly motivates me, gives my life significance, and allows me to be part of something greater than myself.

One of the moments that led me to believe in this change was when I was deciding on what career path I wanted to take. I had two options in front of me. One was a well-paying corporate existence that could give me security, respect, and material comforts. The alternative was a career in an industry that I cared about but was less secure and earned less money. The old me would not have had a doubt; I would have taken the most profitable option, thinking that success was achieved through earning vast amounts of money. But the new me? The person who had discovered that experiences, joy, and helping others were all far more vital? He did doubt.

For the first time, I didn't ask myself, "What will I get paid for?" but "What career will allow me to wake up every morning feeling excited about the day?" I weighed everything I had learned—the fortitude from trying and failing, the fulfillment from acquiring knowledge, and the joy of meaningfully touching people's lives.

And when I framed the choice in those terms, the choice was easy.

I chose passion over prestige. I chose purpose over predictability. And never have I regretted it.

I've learned that success is not a destination—it's a moving target, a highly personal journey that changes as you change. Nowadays, success means waking up excited, working on things I care about, and living a life congruent with what I know. It's being here today, not always looking to climb up the next ladder rung. It's about creating definitions on my terms, not having the world define what I want.

In my humble opinion, success is highly individualistic. Some succeed at getting rich, some at obtaining freedom to create, some by helping others, and some by discovering an adventurous life. There is no single formula for success—it has only the one you construct yourself.

If I had to leave one thing behind from what I've learned, it would be this: don't let the world define success for you. Define it for yourself. Because the thing is, when you're in bed at the end of your life, looking back on what you've done, you won't be thinking about the balance in your bank account or the titles on your CV. You will remember the good and bad days, the things that molded you into who you are, and the mark you left upon the world. And that? That itself is the real success.

Chapter 8: Financial Wisdom

Before I left for the States, I used to look at money as simply working for it, earning it and spending it, and hopefully having enough left over to live on comfortably. At home, elders make financial decisions. My parents took care of the oversized- budget items, and I never had to concern myself with essentials like rent, utilities, or groceries. The mall allowances I earned through my internship and monthly allowances were saved in my checking account, and I used them extravagantly without even caring about budgeting. My concept of being financially responsible was going out and spending money stupidly, but I never considered keeping an eye on my expenses or saving in the long term.

That fantasy was dispelled the moment I entered my new foreign existence. For the first time, I was solely in charge of my finances, and I didn't know how to manage such a privilege. The freedom thrilled me. I could now purchase whatever I desired, dine out whenever I chose, and spend money without explaining it to anyone. It was initially freeing, but I was in financial trouble without knowing it.

My initial financial mistake was underestimating the cost of living. Before leaving home, I had made rough calculations based on rent, school fees, and food prices. I had not anticipated the hidden expenses: transportation, textbooks, laundry, and groceries that never lasted as long as I thought they would, and little by little, these expenditures added up. The first few weeks, I spent money the way I always had, without constantly monitoring my bank balance. I would purchase coffee at expensive shops, get takeout whenever I did not feel like cooking, and indulge in items I did not necessarily require.

Initially, I rationalized these expenses to myself: "I deserve this. I'm abroad, experiencing new things." I convinced myself that spending money was part of "making the most of the experience." But a month later, I started noticing a terrifying pattern. My bank balance was rapidly decreasing, and I had no idea why. I had enough saved up for the semester, but I had already spent a bunch of it.

The harsh reality struck me when I opened my banking app one day and realized how poor I was. My heart sank. How did I end up so far in so short a time? I had no budget plan or financial boundaries—I was just spending without any proper plan. The possibility of going bankrupt terrified me. I had always taken pride in being responsible, but now reality hit me in the face: I had been irresponsible with money, and unless I changed my habits soon, I would be in trouble.

That was my wake-up call. I understood that financial freedom is not about having money but managing it well. The following day, I sat down with my receipts and tallied up all the money I had spent last month. Seeing those figures in black and white was appalling. Hundreds of dollars were spent on impulse buys, unnecessary restaurant meals, and amusement. I realized that I could have saved up so much money had I been financially aware. For a minute, it looked like my financial future was in jeopardy.

This error imparted my first good lesson about financial sense: just because you have money doesn't mean you necessarily have to spend it. What matters isn't how much you make but how well you manage what you already have.

Bad monetary habits are slippery slopes, and it's difficult to stop once you begin to slide. For most young adults and students, it starts with tiny luxuries: a $5 latte here, a superfluous Uber ride there, a gadget that wasn't even needed. These don't look like high-budget items by themselves, but sooner or later, they add up to an insurmountable mountain of financial pressure.

My bad spending habits caught up with me early on. Once I saw that I was overspending, I adjusted but wasn't disciplined yet. I convinced myself I was being clever, but I hadn't created a structured method for managing money. That is when I caught one of the deadliest financial pitfalls overseas: overspending due to peer pressure.

During college, a silent social expectation exists to hang out and eat at any opportunity. It is very convenient to catch oneself exclaiming, "Everyone does it, and therefore I'm doing it." Whenever my peers needed to head out for drinks or whenever they were ordering delivery instead of preparing food, I barely denied them. However, I recognized that it wasn't an imperative cost. I did not want to be someone who never accepted invitations because of financial constraints.

The trap of the credit card came later. The first thing I did when I arrived was apply for a student credit card. I used it sensibly at first, but soon, it became a convenient means of postponing any financial responsibility. If I didn't have sufficient funds in my checking account, I'd simply charge it on the credit card—vowing to pay it off someday. I hadn't anticipated how rapidly credit card balances add up and how risky it is to pay high interest rates if you don't pay the balance in full every month.

The financial crisis hit when I couldn't afford to pay my rent. It was the worst wake-up call possible. I gawked at my bank statement, tallying past-due bills and agonizing over whether or not I'd have to beg my parents for money. The possibility was humiliating. I had left home with the assurance that I would be independent and not depend on my parents anymore. But I was in trouble because I had been irresponsible with money.

That night, I sat down and studied my expenses closely. I reviewed each expense, especially noting the unnecessary ones. I saw a trend: mindless spending, shopping on impulse, and overreliance on credit. I had been blowing money, figuring that financial security would come magically. You must be intentional with money, or things will be out of your hands.

The experience also taught me another vital lesson: financial security is not having a lot of money but being responsible with what you have. I had been making enough to live well, but my failure to plan left me in a lurch.

Then, I vowed never to let monetary concerns control me again. I set a firm budget, monitored every dollar I spent, and set limits on how much cash I could waste on luxuries. Most of all, I no longer consider what other people think about my finances. If I couldn't afford it, I refused. If I was compelled to cook instead of ordering takeout, I did. Money was more important than temporary pleasure.

The hardest part of financial mistakes isn't losing money—it's the stress, pressure, and feeling of losing control. But the best part is that they can be corrected. The secret is to learn from them before they become habits.

I realized that I was at the edge of a financial crisis. It was an awakening I couldn't possibly disregard. I had spent my first few months abroad splurging, money being a bottomless pit for me, and not paying attention to where the money went. The consequences were brutal on me. I barely had enough left to cover my rent, my credit card debt was soaring, and I finally knew what it was like to be financially at risk for the first time. It wasn't about money anymore; it was about being in control, taking responsibility, and caring for myself without relying on emergency aid.

That's when I realized I needed a financial system. I had to be careful, disciplined, and strategic about every dollar I spent. I started learning about budgeting, saving, and conscious spending—something I had always known but needed practice.

1. The First Step: Creating a Budget That Works

I first sorted my finances into specific categories. Previously, I'd never paid much attention to where I spent my money. Rent was an easy-to-grasp cost, but the rest? A haze. Food, transportation, fun, subscriptions—all mixed in my mind, and I had no idea how much I was truly spending.

I created a straightforward system: Essentials, Non-Essentials, and Savings.

- Essentials → Rent, food, tuition, transport, telephone, and utility bills.
- Non-Essentials → Eating out, entertainment, shopping, subscription services, and travel.
- Savings → Some portion of whatever remained after the bills.

I needed to save a bit each month for the very first time in:

- Save money for necessities first,
- Reduce unnecessary spending,
- Save some amount—anything—into the savings. I used an easy 50-30-20 rule initially:
- 50% to necessities (since rent and school fees were non-negotiable).
- 30% was to go towards personal spending (but needed to prioritize what had to be purchased).
- 20% was to savings (even small, but had to begin somehow).

The hardest part was staying on plan. Budgeting doesn't work unless you follow through, so I forced myself to check my finances once a week, no matter what. I'd review my expenses line by line to ensure they were not getting out of hand. It was time-consuming at first, but before long, I noticed something remarkable: I spent less naturally by being conscious of how I spent money.

2. Need vs. Want: Smarter Money Choices

After setting my budget, I had to work on another problem: avoiding spending money on things I didn't have to. The problem wasn't that I was spending money but on the wrong things.

Whenever I reached for my wallet, I asked myself a simple question: Is this a need or a want?

- Need → Something one needs to survive or sustain health for the long term (rent, food, transportation).
- Want → Something that gives short-term pleasure but is unnecessary (daily Starbucks, impulse buying, weekend trips at a high cost).

Before I would ever make a purchase, I would pause and reflect:

- Do I need this, or do I just want it now?
- If I buy this, will I be sorry at the end of the month?
- Is there a cheaper or more innovative way to fulfill this demand?

For instance, I spent $5 on coffee every morning—$150 a month before learning about appropriate money management. When I calculated the numbers, I was appalled. Could I make coffee at home for a percentage of what it costs at the store? Sure, and I did.

Another was dining out. It was convenient, but it cost as much money to dine out once as it did to buy three days' worth of groceries. I made a deal with myself: I could dine out once a week, but the rest had to be made at home.

Although these small things didn't amount to much initially, they saved hundreds of dollars.

3. Tracking Every Expense: The Life-Saver

Soon enough, I learned that it disappears unless you track your money.

So, I started using a budgeting tool (Mint, YNAB, and PocketGuard, which works well) to categorize my expenses. I keyed in cash spending into the tool. By the end of each week, I reviewed my expenditure pattern and adjusted my budget accordingly.

For non-app individuals, a simple spreadsheet works just as well. I created a Google Sheet with the following columns:

- Date (when I spent it)
- Category (food, rent, transport, etc.)
- Amount spent
- Reason for spending

What is the most significant benefit of expense tracking? I became hyper-aware of wasteful spending. I forced myself to cut back if I realized I had already spent too much on non-necessities for the month.

4. The Turning Point: Financial Discipline and Stability

Three months later, I got the first proof that my plan was working. For the first time since leaving overseas, I wasn't fretting about cash at the end of the month. I had enough to pay rent without anxiety, had some savings (although small), and ended my paycheck-to-paycheck existence.

I also felt a change in attitude. Rather than spending money frivolously, I prioritized financial stability. Having a sense of mastery over my money was liberating—it no longer controlled me; I controlled it.

One day, a surprise medical bill hit. Usually, this would have sent me into a panic, and I would have scrambled to find the money. But this time, I had an emergency fund. I paid the bill quietly and without stress, and in that instant, I finally understood financial stability.

. It was realizing that regardless, I was in charge of my money, not the reverse.
By the time I regained control of my finances, I knew something valuable: it's not how you escape a financial disaster; it's how you make sure you never get into one in the first place. Financial discipline is like learning a new language; it initially feels clumsy but soon becomes second nature.

The most significant difference in my journey wasn't budgeting or keeping track of expenses. Still, as much as the good money habits I developed, I discovered that managing money isn't about depriving yourself but making conscious choices that serve your objectives.

1. The Power of Small but Impactful Changes

Financial security comes from extreme changes, such as new jobs, significant investments, or eliminating huge spending categories. However, the most beneficial changes are small, incremental ones. Here are some of the best money management changes I made:

- Cutting Down Eating Out: Instead of eating out, I started cooking. Easy foods like pasta, stir-fries, or sandwiches saved me hundreds of dollars monthly.

- Canceling Unnecessary Subscriptions: I had subscribed to a few streaming platforms, a gym I barely used, and an online magazine I barely read. Canceling unnecessary subscriptions released money in the meantime.
- More brilliant Grocery Shopping: I started meal planning instead of impulse shopping. I shopped intentionally, weekly rather than daily, and opted for inexpensive yet healthy foods.
- Using Public Transport Rather than Rideshares: I used to take Uber for quick trips and/or convenience, but taking public transport and cycling saved me significantly more each month.
- Each of these changes seemed insignificant, but they altered my financial situation.

2. Earning and Saving While Studying or Working Abroad

Managing expenses is only half the solution. The other half is learning how to increase income.
Below are some ways I and others successfully earned and saved abroad:

- Part-Time Employment: Most universities allow international students to work part-time. Working in offices, cafés, or libraries is an ideal way to earn money without affecting studies.
- Freelancing: I met students who earned money online by tutoring, graphic design, writing, and coding. These students gained knowledge through Upwork, Fiverr, and TutorMe platforms.

- Internships: Instead of looking solely for unpaid internships, I searched for paid ones—even lower-paying than a corporate sector job, but I made money and gained experience.
- Selling Old Items: Instead of accumulating worthless clothes, books, and electronics, I sold them through online marketplaces or student bazaars. This cleared out space and made me extra money.
- Grants and Scholarships: A few schools offer merit- or need-based financial aid that can reduce tuition. I found that it doesn't pay to be timid!

These options weren't exclusively centered on making money; they helped me create financial autonomy.

3. Real-Life Applications of Financial Frugality Abroad

My most memorable

experience was working with students who had developed financial discipline from day one. This experience taught me that good money habits lead to long-term success.

Example 1: Raj – The Frugal Saver

Raj, my friend from India, who is currently in the U.S., is very disciplined about his finances. He has a straightforward rule: "Save before you spend." Instead of reducing his savings proportionate to his expenses, he did just the opposite—first, he saved a certain amount and altered his lifestyle based on that.

This meant no frivolous spending, dining at home rather than dining out, and avoiding short-term pleasure for long-term stability. By the time he graduated, Raj had saved up enough to finance his move to his first job without relying on his family's support.

Example 2: Julia – The Freelancer Who Paid Off Her Tuition

Julia, an exchange student from Germany, started working online as a language tutor and content writer. At first, she did it for extra money, but she soon realized she could use this income to cover a large portion of her tuition fees.

Instead of spending money on extravagance, she worked hard and saved it. By the time she left university, she had almost no debt and had saved for future vacations.

Example 3: Ethan – The Shrewd Investor

Ethan, my American classmate, started investing early. He didn't invest in big trades; he invested small amounts in stocks and index funds every month. While we were still trying to understand budgeting, he already had an investment portfolio.

These people showed me that it's not luck with financial discipline but attitude and strategy.

4. My Personal Financial Turnaround

My financial makeover didn't happen overnight. It took months of trial and error, self-discipline, and learning from my mistakes. But once I started making smarter money decisions, I felt a sense of control I never had before.

Instead of stressing about money, I felt confident about my financial future. I no longer feared the end of the month because I knew I had a plan.

This is how I changed:

- I tracked every expense, so blind spending was a thing of the past. Now, I always knew where my money was going.
- I made thoughtful purchases. Every expense was intentional, not spontaneous.
- I focused on financial growth. Instead of just saving, I started investing, considering career advancement opportunities and side hustles.
- I prioritized financial independence. I made sure that I never had to borrow for essential expenses again.

After my second year abroad, I realized I had accomplished something meaningful: establishing a basis of financial stability.

By the time I had built better financial habits, I felt something I hadn't in years—control. I no longer have last-minute worries about rent, I no longer feel shame after impulse purchases, and I no longer feel like my money would slip through my fingers. But as I became more stable, another question started looming: What's next?

Focusing on short-term financial survival is easy when you're a student or a young professional, but what about the bigger picture? Financial security isn't just about staying afloat—it's about planning for the future. And that's where long-term financial planning comes in.

1. Balancing Ambition with Financial Responsibility

One key thing I learned is that financial planning is not about giving up ambition but about maintaining it. I used to think of success as chasing the most significant opportunities, which could be the best jobs, investments, or companies. However, even the most critical opportunities become costly liabilities without financial security.

For example, I have a friend, Aaron, who landed a much-coveted job in a big city after graduating from university. He was earning an excellent salary, but he did the typical thing of spending too much too soon, renting a fancy apartment, leasing a new vehicle, and blowing money like there was no tomorrow because he felt he had "made it." A year later, he was living paycheck to paycheck despite earning more than most people our age. His drive wasn't the problem—his failure to budget was.

Then, I realized the smartest professionals weren't the ones chasing money. They were those who let money work for them. They spent less than they earned, invested aggressively, and made decisions based on long-term goals rather than short-term gratification.

So, I asked myself how I reconcile career ambition with financial security.?

- Live like a student even when you earn money. Just because you make more money doesn't mean you need to spend more.

- Don't fall into the trap of lifestyle inflation. Your first big paycheck is not an invitation to increase your lifestyle—think long-term.
- Separate career goals from financial needs. Just because an opportunity is exciting doesn't mean it's financially savvy. Weigh risks carefully.
- Plan your finances with the future in mind. A great career means nothing if you're drowning in debt or financial stress.

2. Smart Money Management for the Future

Once I committed to long-term financial stability, I had to set a strong economic base to support my plans.

Key things I realized regarding long-term financial management:

- Developing Credit Responsibly
  One of the first things I learned is that credit isn't the issue; bad credit practices are. Some people avoid credit cards entirely because they don't want to owe money, but responsibly using credit builds credibility with your money. I did these things:
  I paid off my credit card balance within a month.
  Had a low credit utilization rate (less than 30%).
  I never borrowed money and could not reasonably repay it quickly.
- Avoid Bad Debt:
  Good debt (like education loans with low interest) can be an investment for the future. Bad debt (like high-interest credit card

debt) is a money trap. I promised never to borrow money unless I had a clear plan to repay it.

- Start a Savings Plan Early:
  The best financial tip I ever received was to start saving when you think you don't have to. Although it was only a fraction of my salary, saving monthly money helped me build economic security one step at a time.
- Understanding Investing
  Savings are significant, but investing makes money flourish. I started learning about index funds, mutual funds, and long-term investments to ensure that my savings were not just idle but benefiting me.

3. Financial Planning for Young Professionals

When I graduated from student to working life, I realized that money management doesn't end with budgeting; it expands with life. The choices I made now would determine my financial stability later in life.
These are the things I learned in planning for the next phase of life:

- Learning about Taxes
  I didn't realize how complicated taxes were until I had to prepare my first foreign tax return. Understanding deductions, tax brackets, and clever tax-saving techniques ahead of time kept me from making blunders that many young professionals make.
- Saving for Future Education or Career Changes
  Most young professionals land themselves having spent all their money without preparedness for unplanned opportunities.

Continuing education, certification, or switching jobs were among the possibilities that I could do without fear of worrying about finances due to my economic cushion.

- Having sound career decisions
  It's simple enough to chase after the highest-paying job, but I learned to look past the paycheck and consider other factors like stability, benefits, and work-life balance. Taking a slightly lower-paying job with long-term potential can often be better than a higher-paying job with little stability.

4. Last Insight: Money as a Tool, Not an Object

After so many years of struggling, learning, and ending up financially independent, I picked up something significant:

Financial independence is not being wealthy. It's being the master of your money, so your money is not the master of you.

At one point in my life, I thought success was determined by how much money I earned. Today, I understand that success is all about financial peace of mind—feeling prepared for the unexpected, not constantly stressed about money, and being able to make decisions without financial desperation leading my choices.

Looking back, my worst financial blunders weren't so much that I overspent as I didn't have a plan. Financial security is built on intelligent habits, self-discipline, and intentional choices.

If I had one piece of advice to offer to anyone struggling to manage finances abroad, it would be this:
Seize your financial future as an investment. Every wise decision you make today, saving, budgeting, or avoiding unnecessary debt, is a step toward a future where money works for you, not against you.

Financial savvy isn't about limitation. It's about freedom. It's about confidence that you'll be financially prepared for whatever life brings. That's true success.

Chapter 9: Resilience Through Setbacks

Managing Professional Disappointments – Short of Job Expectations

The first professional disappointment I experienced left me feeling like the rug had been pulled from under my feet. I had always believed that hard work was the sole factor that would result in success. I had done everything I thought I needed, obtained relevant education skills, and networked with the right people for my career. But when the opportunity to get a good job arose, I was outside looking in.

The process was off to a good start. I had spent weeks perfecting my resume, practicing interview techniques, and canvassing for companies. One particular position was extremely desirable for me—a luxury company in my field was looking for fresh talent. The position suited my skills, the company culture was ideal, and I had survived the initial screening phases unscathed.

When I got to the final rounds of interviews, I was optimistic but nervous. The interviewers were executive directors, and I highlighted my strengths, problem-solving capacity, and passion. I stepped out of the room with hope, already envisioning working there, contributing, and growing in my career.

And then, the email.

"We appreciate your time and interest in our organization. But we have selected other applicants who are currently a more suitable fit for the role."

I read the words repeatedly, hoping I had misunderstood them. My stomach was in knots. I hadn't been good enough.

The Frustration and Self-Doubt of Rejection

At first, I brushed it off, believing it was nothing. "It's just one job. I'll get the next one." But with every rejection that came after, doubt crept in. Was I not as talented as I thought? Had I overestimated my abilities? Was I even in the right line of work?

I remember sitting in my tiny apartment, looking at the screen of my laptop, trying to wrap my head around it. I had worked so hard, so why didn't that count? My peers were getting jobs, their success being heralded on LinkedIn, and I was at the starting line, sitting back and allowing everyone else to get on with it.

The more I dwelled on it, the madder I became. I found myself questioning all of my past decisions. Should I have studied something else? Should I have started networking earlier? Should I have focused on certifications rather than marks? The act of questioning my judgment was killing me.

Worst of all, I was silenced after being rejected. Most employers left explanations behind: "We've chosen another candidate." "We're looking elsewhere." Whatever it stated left me at a loss. Was it a lack of experience?

Interview performance? Qualifications? Without constructive feedback, I had no negotiating power to build on.

Considering Alternative Options

For weeks, I struggled with doubt. I started avoiding talking about job hunting with friends and loved ones. Every time someone inquired, "So, have you received any job offers yet?" I felt guilty. The pressure I put on myself and the invisible peer pressure felt like something was suffocating me.

I had reached a point where I considered dropping the course of study I wanted to take. I wasn't the right fit for it. It felt like it was time to do something else and move in another direction. The thought of changing my career path felt like an admission of failure, but at that moment, I was desperate for anything that didn't feel like another dead end.

But unbeknownst to everyone else, I knew leaving was not an option. I just had to find another way to cope.

And this was when I realized that I must learn through my failures and not merely exist through them.

I went over my applications and looked for answers:

- What were the careers that I was applying for?
- What were they persistently asking that I lacked?
- Where was I missing the mark?

There was a definite trend. I had interviewed for most of the jobs that required more experience than I possessed. I had the education, the academic training, and the motivation, but companies wanted proof that I could apply the skills to real-world circumstances.

That was an eye-opener. I had been so caught up with job searching that I had not noticed the absence of gaps in my experiential background. Instead of moving in the same direction, I had to re-strategize.

For the first time, I had allowed myself to view a failure differently- not as a personal attack but as proof of what I had to mend. Instead of taking rejection as the end, I saw it as a blueprint—a map of where I had to reach. That was the beginning of a resilient and structured approach toward job applications..

Professional mistakes were one thing, but failure on a personal level hurt far more. No rejection letter or job application denied could be more horrific than the loneliness, self-doubt, and emotional drain caused by failure in my own life.

Living abroad had afforded me independence, self-discipline, and potential, but it had also isolated me from those I had always known as my comfort zone. No matter how diligently I toiled to focus on building my career, issues concerning myself always cropped up, causing me to doubt my decisions, abilities, and even my place in the world.

The Weight of Homesickness and Loneliness

The first few months after immigrating overseas had been surprisingly challenging. Everything was new—a new town, new people, new experiences. But as the high wore off, harsh reality dawned. The people I had known since childhood, the always present family, and the friends with whom I could hang out at any moment were all lost.

Nobody prepares you for the deafening silence of being alone in an apartment thousands of miles from home, wondering if you have made the right choice. The late-night calls with my family were reassuring but reminded me of what I was missing. Festivals, birthdays, family reunions; life moved on and did not wait for me.

And then there were the foreign friendships. While I had friends, foreign friendships were different. People came and went, but the deep emotional bonds I'd formed with people from home were more slowly established in this new life.

A Relationship That Didn't Work Out

I endured a relationship that ended even before it had grown. For a moment, I had found someone who made the distance and loneliness bearable. She understood the frustration of being away from home, the exhaustion of trying to stay current on all things, and the fear of trying to grasp life in a new place.

But eventually, we both realized that we had our problems. The demands of college life, money troubles, and emotional exhaustion started taking their toll, and instead of clinging to each other, we started drifting away from each other.

I tried to persevere, but sometimes, despite your efforts, things aren't meant to happen as they should. When it didn't work, I felt like I had failed again—albeit this time, not for grades, jobs, or professional goals. This time, it was about fitting in, feeling connected, and being significant to someone.

Comparing Myself to Peers

The ghastly part of lagging on the personal front was watching everybody else succeed. I was being rejected at jobs and brokenhearted, while my friends were getting ahead by seemingly effortless measures. Careers, stable relationships, breakthroughs—social media was an entire album of people getting ahead while I earned nothing.

I was second-guessing myself. Was I the problem? Was I just not working hard enough? Was I just not qualified enough?

The more I compared myself to everyone else, the worse I felt. But I did not realize then that no one blogs about their failure. Everyone simply blogs about the highlights of their life, the things that work, and the perfect photograph. Everyone has their failures; they simply don't post them.

That would become clear later on. That time, I simply felt behind.

But I did not realize then that failure does not always equate to setbacks but to growth.

Turning Failures into Moments of Learning

Something had to change. I was tired of feeling like I was losing. Along the way, I realized that failures would not stop. I could allow them to define me or learn from them.

I started viewing failures differently. Instead of seeing them as a door slammed shut in my face, I saw them as an arrow pointing to something I hadn't considered before.

Failure is a Teacher

The more I looked into it, the more I noticed patterns in my failures:

- I wasn't getting hired because I lacked experience.
- I was lonely because I wasn't genuinely attempting to build authentic connections.
- My relationship ended because I was waiting for the other person to fill the emotional space I had left vacant within myself.

It was a bitter pill, but setbacks weren't happening to me—they were trying to transform me. They highlighted areas that I needed to improve, areas that I had been avoiding.

I stopped wondering, "Why is this happening to me?" and wondered, "What is this trying to teach me?"

A Setback That Led to an Unexpected Opportunity

The biggest shock was one of the rejections that ultimately proved an opportunity for tremendous growth.

After I applied, I received a couple of rejections, so I started looking for opportunities elsewhere. My friend suggested I take a consulting internship not included in my original career path. I was not very interested at first. It was not my dream job or within the industry, I was searching for.

But with my past failures, I felt like I had nothing to lose.

I applied, got the interviews, and, to my utter surprise, I was accepted.

What I never expected was that this was going to be a turnaround in everything.

- The work taught me new things I never thought I would ever need.
- It provided me with a mentor who helped me obtain better employment.
- It gave me the confidence in my skills that I had previously overlooked.

I would never have had this new opportunity if I had been working in the job I initially wanted.

That is when it struck me: sometimes, getting rejected takes you to something better.

The Power of Self-Reflection and Re-Evaluating Goals

Then, every time there was a setback, I practiced self-reflection.
I would ask myself:

- What did I learn through this process?
- What would I do differently the next time?
- Was I even going in the right direction, to begin with, or was I pushing something that wasn't supposed to be mine?

Instead of forcing my way past obstacles, I started working around them.
Instead of seeing failure as a stop sign, I started seeing failure as a redirection toward something better.

Not getting hired meant figuring out how to do the job better.
Breaking up with her required focusing on self-development.
Being single requires intentionally establishing more secure relationships.

I stopped being terrified of failure and started to learn from it.
Finally, I learned what resilience is.

Strategies for Staying Motivated During Setbacks

Setbacks, failures, and disappointments are inevitable. No matter how much we plan, things won't always go as planned. The real test isn't avoiding failure—it's learning to keep going when it happens.

When I'd experienced my share of setbacks—rejected job prospects, personal setbacks, and broken expectations—I had two choices:

- Let setbacks define me.
- Use them as fuel to keep going.

The second route wasn't easy, but it was the only path. That's what I realized about staying motivated when life's plans fail.

1. The Power of Reframing Failures

One of the most significant mental shifts I have made was learning how to reframe failure, to stop viewing it as an end, and to start viewing it as a lesson.

Instead of asking, "Why did this happen to me?" I asked myself, "What can I learn from this?"

For example, after applying for a series of jobs only to be turned down, I came to learn that:

- I didn't lack ability; I lacked experience.
- I wasn't unqualified; I just needed some expertise to be better qualified.
- Rejections weren't evidence of failure; they were indicators instructing me on how to improve.

This slight change in mindset was what made all the difference. Each failure became a stepping stone rather than an obstacle.

2. Setting Small, Achievable Goals to Regain Confidence

When things don't go as planned, it's easy to get in over one's head. The solution? Start small.

Instead of attempting enormous, intimidating goals (like getting my ideal job immediately), I set tiny, achievable steps:

- Learn a new skill within my industry.
- Apply for one job daily instead of letting rejection paralyze me.
- Network with at least one new professional every week.

Every small victory gained momentum. Rather than dwelling on everything I hadn't done, I began concentrating on what I could do.

3. Building a Strong Support Network

Setbacks are immensely alienating.. That is why you need the right people by your side.

One of the most significant errors I made early on was attempting to do everything myself. I believed that seeking assistance made me weak or incompetent. But I learned that strong individuals don't accomplish things alone. They construct robust support networks.

- Friends constantly reminded me that failure is temporary.
- Mentors offered guidance and insights I never thought of.
- Networking brought me into contact with others who had experienced similar failures and bounced back.

The individuals around me kept reminding me of my potential whenever I felt like quitting.

4. The Mindset Shift: Setbacks Don't Define Success

One of the most consistent lies in popular culture is that one never fails on the way to success. Success is knowing how to get up after having fallen. The most successful individuals I've ever known shared one thing in common: they'd failed more than they'd succeeded, but they'd never quit.

When I understood this, I lost my fear of failure. Instead of viewing it as something preventing me from succeeding, I began viewing it as a part of the journey.

The Ultimate Takeaway—Resilience as a Skill

Reflecting on all of the failures that happened to me, I now know that every one of those failures molded me into the person I am today.

At the time, each failure seemed like the world had ended. In retrospect, however, they were the best things that ever happened.

- Each obstacle caused me to keep moving forward.
- Each rejection pushed me further to something greater.
- Each failure taught me to be resilient.

Resilience Isn't About Never Failing—It's About Getting Back Up After

As far back as I can remember, I believed resilience meant being strong enough never to fail. I was mistaken.

Resilience is:

- Disappointed but not giving up.
- Rejected and going on anyway.
- Falling behind and still catching up.
- Learning from failure rather than repeating it.

After I revised my definition of resilience, I no longer feared setbacks and began to welcome growth.

Universal Takeaways for Readers—How to Use Resilience in Your Life

If you're experiencing setbacks, keep this in mind:

- Failure does not indicate that you're not good enough; it suggests you're growing.
- Rejection is not personal; it's feedback. Learn from it.

- Setbacks are temporary, but the lessons you learn from them are permanent.
- Don't let doubt keep you back. Keep going even when it's tough.

The truth is nobody achieves success without first experiencing failure. The only distinction between successful and unsuccessful individuals? Successful individuals don't give up.

Final Reflection—The Setback That Changed Everything

If I had received everything I wanted when I wanted it, I would not be where I am today.

Somewhere along the way, I'll look back on my struggles and thank them because they gave me the most significant opportunities, experiences, and education.

And if you're somewhere in a tough place right now, just remember:

Your failure today is making you better for tomorrow.

Chapter 10: A Journey Worth Living

Looking Back on the Journey—From Doubt to Growth

If I could go back in time and speak to my younger self, the one who doubted, the one who second-guessed every step, the one who thought he wouldn't make it through—I'd say to him:

"You're going to be okay."

Because, at first, I wasn't so sure that I was.

When I went abroad for the first time, I didn't simply pack my bag. I packed questions, uncertainty, and hope. Would I get there? Was I doing the right thing? Was I enough? I didn't have comforting answers. I didn't know anything except that I was venturing into the unknown, and the looming shadow of failure hung over me.

The Struggles That Shaped Me

Some challenges in every stage of my life pushed me to the breaking point.

- Denial of my capabilities.
- Managing my finances as an international student.
- Personal setbacks, which made me question my priorities.

Back then, all of them appeared to be signs to quit. Yet today, I know that all these second-guessing and experiences conditioned my mindset and ultimately shaped me into the person I am today.

The Transformation: From Doubt to Confidence

In those early months abroad, I was guarded, anxious, and fearful of messing up. I was often fixated on the negatives, afraid of losing, being strange, and being different.

Life isn't that kind, though. Despite your complaints, it pushes you to grow out of your shell and learn.

Along the way, I conquered my fear of failure and learned to enjoy the lessons that it provided. I learned to say yes to those opportunities I once said no to. I learned to stop waiting for the "right " moment and began creating my timeline.

- I discovered how to venture out and obtain a job even when I was not 100% qualified.
- I learned how to be efficient in financial management..
- I learned that losses were not dead ends but secret beginnings.

There was a time when I knew I was no longer the timid, fearful person I once was. Instead, I was a person who stood tall in the face of challenges, a person who knew in their bones that failure was not the denial of success but a part of it.

A Moment of Epiphany—How Far I Had Come

One of the defining moments of accepting my proposal was re-reading an email from the archives..

It was from one of the many companies I had applied to, one of the many rejections that had pounded my morale into pulp back then. That email would have been proof that I was not good enough. But sitting here, reading it today, I could only feel gratitude.

Because since then, I'd:

- I gained skills I never dreamed of having.
- Established a career to be proud of.
- Overcome financial difficulties that previously had appeared to be insurmountable.
- Became more self-sufficient and developed a robust sense of self.

That rejection had once been a slammed door. But I now knew that it had propelled me toward more significant things.

Another thing that helped me through the process was having coffee with a mentor who had supported me during some of my lowest points. I explained that I was stuck, and he smiled and said, "You don't even realise how far you've come, do you?"

For the first time, I was frozen..

The barriers which had seemed impossible to overcome were now stepping stones. The vulnerabilities which had caused me to be afraid in the past had strengthened me even more.

I had changed from an individual who was afraid of the unknown to one who loved the journey, regardless of where it may lead.

There's a myth that you're successful if you never fail, you do everything just right, work your butt off, and work it all out. But life has a strange way of surprising yo u as it rarely goes according to plan.

Why Resilience is the Key to Success

In retrospect, I see now that the defining moments in my life were not when things were working out, but when they weren't. Each failure, each rejection, each monetary emergency presented me with a choice:

- Let it burden me and make me anxious and fearful.
- Or learn how to accept the challenge head-on.

For a long time, I believed resilience meant being wise enough never to get into a mess. I was wrong, though. Resilience isn't about not messing up, but what you do when that happens.

- Every time it messed up, I learned a new skill/lesson.
- Every time that I failed, I was redirected to something better..
- Each obstacle brought out a new facet in my personality.

Adaptation as a Survival Mechanism

I realised that if resilience is the centre of persistence, then flexibility is the essential cog in the wheel ..

Adjusting to life in another country was the most significant adaptation I ever had to make. Everything was new—the culture, the school, the money, I had to accustom myself to a new world and deal with the pressure of success.

- Cultural adaptation—new habits learned, and bridging the communication gap.
- Surviving with minimal funds—finally learning the meaning of a "hand-to-mouth existence..

- Dealing with career failure—learning to adapt when it didn't work.

Adjustment was not an option; it was the need of the hour..

A Turning Point: The Challenges That Shaped My Success

I have come a long way because I was hired to do a job that was once totally out of my league.

I'd attempted to get work with a large company the year before, and they'd rejected me. They wanted work experience and qualifications I didn't have then. As another door closed, the feeling that I wasn't worthy intensified.

But after a year of learning, adjusting, and developing a solid skillset, I reapplied. This time, I was more confident, with more experience and a better idea of what I could bring.

And this time?

I landed the job.

It wasn't so much about getting the job as it was about understanding that the individual rejected a year ago was now a different person altogether, not the same one applying now.

The difficulties I had overcome, the obstacles I had surmounted, and the wisdom I had gained had readied me for this day..

I realised something significant: I still won despite all the challenges and downfalls.

Redefining Success—More Than Simply Money or Prestige

I have always defined success in terms of money.

- A fat bank account.
- An executive position.

I was grossly mistaken. As I progressed in my journey, something changed. The things that I used to think would make me successful weren't the things that brought me joy.

The Evolution of My Perception of Success

At first, success was all about money and stability. I was taught when I was young that financial security was the key to success: a stable career, a regular paycheck, and a comfortable life.

Then, I began to encounter people who defined success differently.

- Some defined success in terms of experiences.
- Some defined it in terms of relationships and connections.
- Some quantified it as freedom, doing what they enjoyed without being bound by society's expectations.

It made me rethink everything.

What if success wasn't money but being able to live a life that satisfied me?

What if it was waking up looking forward to the day instead of counting down to the end of work?

Why True Success is Measured in Fulfilment, Not Just Achievements

I knew that a lucrative career translates to nothing if you are unhappy. That external validation —in the form of titles, status, accolades—is fleeting.

Real success shines from within.

- It's waking up with a sense of fulfilment, not just running after a salary.
- It's establishing meaningful relationships, not pursuing superficial status.

For me, that meant refocusing.

- I no longer compare myself to others. Their journey was not mine, and their vision of success wasn't mine.
- I began to focus on what truly brought me joy—work, people who motivated me, and a lifestyle that made me feel alive.
- I no longer measured success by numbers; instead, I measured it by growth.

Ultimately, you can have all the things you ever dreamed of and needed and still be hollow. Being successful is based on a foundation of passion and inner peace.

A Moment of Realisation: What Felt Like Failure Was Truly Redirection

One of the most significant shifts in my life was the result of a failure that, looking back, was a blessing.

There was a job I had worked towards—one that was the best fit, in my mind, one that would be the career-defining win. When I didn't get it, I was crushed.

I took it as evidence that I wasn't good enough.

But a few months later, a better opportunity came up, one I would not have considered if I had succeeded in getting the initial job.

And I realised something life-altering in that instant:

- At times, what appears to be failure is redirection.
- Sometimes, doors are closed so that better ones can be opened.
- And sometimes, what we want isn't really what we need.

That insight turned everything around.

The biggest lesson I've learned in my journey is this: no one has it all figured out.

- Not the people who are excelling in their careers.
- Not the ones who always appear confident and in control.
- Not even the ones who have achieved "success" by traditional standards.

Life is unpredictable, and everyone is figuring this out on their own

If there's one thing I want readers to learn from my experiences, it's this: You don't need to get all the answers immediately. Some answers come to you quietly, some in a burst of clarity, and both greatly alter your perception of life.

1. Take Bold Steps, Even If You're Afraid

Fear holds more people back than failure ever will.

- Fear of making the wrong choice.
- Fear of failing.
- Fear of what others will think.

But here's the reality: the only way to go forward is to take the first step, even when you're afraid.

I used to overthink and believe I needed to be sure before taking action. But I've realised that certainty never precedes action; it follows. You only become confident by doing, failing, learning, and repeating.

The scariest decisions I made, like moving overseas, sending out resumes for jobs I wasn't exceptionally qualified for, and stepping outside my comfort zone, shaped my future.

So, if you're facing a decision and wondering what to do, take the plunge, even if you're scared.

2. Failures Are Blessings in Disguise—Learn From Them

At one time, I viewed failure as evidence that I wasn't good enough.

Now, I view failure as the most effective teacher I've ever had.

- Failure doesn't mean you're not good enough; it means you're expanding your horizons.
- Every rejection, every setback, every moment of uncertainty is moulding you.
- Rather than shying away from failure, ask: "What is this teaching me?"

When I shifted my perspective, I no longer viewed setbacks as roadblocks and began viewing them as redirections to something greater.

3. Move Forward, Even If You're Not Sure Which Way

There were many times when I felt stuck. I had no idea what my next move should be or whether I was even headed in the right direction.

But I've discovered that success isn't always about having the ideal plan but moving forward.

- Send in your application, even if you're not 100% sure.

- Seize the moment, even if it's not what you had in mind.
- Keep moving, even when you don't have all the answers yet.

The only way to discover clarity is to keep moving. The answers will appear eventually.

4. Your Journey Will Never Look Like Anyone Else's—And That's Okay

It's easy to compare ourselves to others, especially in the age of social media, where everyone seems to be effortlessly achieving success.

But I've realised that no two journeys are the same.

- Some people find success early. Others take longer to figure things out.
- Some follow a traditional path. Others carve out their way.
- Some appear to have it all together. Everyone has things they don't tell you about, though.

The day I stopped comparing my path to others was the day I started growing. So, if you ever feel behind, remember you are right where you are.

A Moment of Connection—Sharing the Lessons

The most satisfying moment in my journey was when I encountered someone facing the same challenges I had faced years earlier.

A recent arrival in the country, a young student, questioning what they wanted to do with their life and grappling with self-doubt, came to me seeking advice.

I saw so much of myself in her.

For the first time, I realised how far I had come. The doubts, struggles, and failures had all led me to where I was now, to the point where I could lead another person.

As I shared my tale with her and reassured her that things would improve, I saw something different in her face. It was a quiet confidence that was not there before.

Then, I understood something important: we don't grow for ourselves. We grow to help others do the same.

A Note of Gratitude and Closing Reflections

Reflecting on this experience, the highs and lows, challenges and triumphs, I know I wasn't alone.

Whatever I've accomplished and however I've survived are because of the people who supported me, believed in me, and pushed me forward even when I doubted myself.

1. Gratitude to the People Who Walked This Journey with Me

- My family stayed with me even when they did not understand my choices.
- My advisers guided me when I was lost.
- My friends stood by me, reminding me I wasn't alone.
- At times, even the obstacles themselves served as my most faithful companions..

I didn't know it at the moment, but every struggle, every obstacle, and failure shaped me into the person I was supposed to be.

And for that, I am deeply grateful.

2. The Journey is Not Over—Growth Never Ceases

The ironic thing about hitting a milestone is that it's never the finish line.

- For every challenge I've overcome, a new one will come.
- For every lesson I've learned, there will be more to discover.
- For every version of myself I've grown into, there's still another version waiting to emerge.

Growth is not a destination; it's a lifelong journey.

And that's what makes life worth living.

3. A Hopeful Ending—Challenging Readers to Accept Their Journey

If you're reading this and are currently experiencing a setback or doubting moment, remember this: it too shall pass.

- You will grow.
- You will move beyond it.
- One day, you'll realise that everything you doubted made you more resolute and strengthened you.

Life is unpredictable, wild, and full of roadblocks, but it's worth living.

4. Last Reflection—Standing in a Position That Once Was Foreign, Now Home

Today, as I sit here typing these lines, I think back to when I first entered this country: scared, uncertain, and unsure of what would happen next.

And now, years later, I stand here in the same place, but all has changed.

Not because the world is different.

But because I am.

The fears that once held me back no longer have power over me.
The weights that once were too heavy for me to carry are lighter than ever..

The doubts that once haunted me have been replaced by confidence.

This place, once foreign, intimidating, and challenging in every way, now feels like home.

And that, most of all, is proof of how far

I've come.

Because, in the end, this trip wasn't about succeeding.

It was about becoming who I was meant to be.

Verses Kindler Publication

Reach us through our website -

https://www.verseskindlerpublication.com/

For more information visit our

Instagram or Facebook page.